MY WISDOM BREATHES

WISDOM ENERGIZES FUN

ROBERT A. WILSON

BALBOA.PRESS

A DIVISION OF HAY HOUSE

This book is a work of non-fiction. Unless otherwise noted, the author and the publisher make no explicit guarantees as to the accuracy of the information contained in this book and in some cases, names of people and places have been altered to protect their privacy.

Balboa Press books may be ordered through booksellers or by contacting:

Balboa Press
A Division of Hay House
1663 Liberty Drive
Bloomington, IN 47403
www.balboapress.com
844-682-1282

The author of this book does not dispense medical advice or prescribe the use of any technique as a form of treatment for physical, emotional, or medical problems without the advice of a physician, either directly or indirectly. The intent of the author is only to offer information of a general nature to help you in your quest for emotional and spiritual well-being. In the event you use any of the information in this book for yourself, which is your constitutional right, the author and the publisher assume no responsibility for your actions.

Print information available on the last page.

ISBN: 978-1-9822-7096-4 (sc)
ISBN: 978-1-9822-7098-8 (hc)
ISBN: 978-1-9822-7097-1 (e)

Library of Congress Control Number: 2021913121

Balboa Press rev. date: 07/13/2021

Contents

May _Cary Strauss's_ life flow
of lavish endless love health wealth fun and cashflow in a beautiful fun

Read this affirmation as you wrote it

I am uniquely beautiful with magical skills thrilling the
cosmos and all people with my unique mystique mystically
and magically expanding thru life in a big bold bright way

Vision Statement

Wisdom Energizing Fun

Mission Statement

My Mission is to open people's enterprising eyes to be liberated from
the past to expand of the now and energize their dreams of the future
with inspirational acuity and integrity to experience being rebelliously
abundant riding your trails of triumph with hypnoacuity while having
fun maturing the unconscious and subconscious celebrations

Thank You for purchasing My Wisdom Breathes

Robert A. Wilson

Information

I placed this information in this information in this book so
people can understand the way the conscious subconscious
and unconscious minds process information

Information for you to open a new understanding about your inner self

The **limbic system** is a set of structures in the brain
that deal with emotions and memory

As the definition of minds are according to
Merriam-Webster Dictionary

Mind as noun: the part of a person that thinks,
reasons, feels, and remembers

Mind as verb: to be bothered by (something): to object to or dislike
(something) to care about or worry about (something or someone).

I now understand and value clearing the way for you to grasp
the deepest parts of the brain contain the hidden challenges
that create our responses to our daily encounters

"Most of our communication is unconscious. Our conscious brain can
only handle roughly like 40 bits of information a second, while our
unconscious minds can handle 11 million bits of data per second."

https://www.forbes.com/sites/nickmorgan/2013/03/07/ -

About the Book

My Wisdom Breathes wisdom inspiration imagination and celebrations
that thrilled my wakeup noo sensing my numinous outlaw optimism
cracking lightning bolt clarity energized my awakened understanding

To fathom and admit the map I embedded from the womb till present
moment are the subconscious unconscious representations feelings
emotions and everything that occurred from the womb till present

Moment that controls and manipulates my life today as I liberated me
from me as I instantly depersonalized my attached emotions making
my past faceless to cut the crap to rap to revolutionize appreciate

Participate and facilitate my personalwised my detached panache to
stop playing the victim as I enterprized my negativity that hastened
my emancipation Zenzation as my au natural now dared me

To dissolve my perfection thinking and tear up my excuseopedia
dissolving all the excuses to stop looking outside myself as I AM
grounded in the poetic power of NO that opened my investors lore

To invest in myself to grasp my life is a mystical mess unsheathed
my listening enthusiasts that personalwised my gunslinger brilliance
accelerated my artistic curiosity triggered my deathless wisdom

That energized my subconscious celebrations introduced me to my
world of words that let fly my rebellious vocabulary that animated my
nunow rave that drew and painted my upshot scenarios that colored

My tabula rasa rapture exalted my spiritual charm to write my
spiritual nowography that illuminated my earthly skies with my bright
rainbow energy animates trailblazer hellraiser enterprising galas

Preface

Read My Wisdom Breathes out loud without trying to know what you're reading to allow yourself the freedom to go on a journey of imaginative inlightenmint that opens your dreams eyes to having fun

My Wisdom Breathes is written in first person with poetic rhymes minimal punctuation politically incorrect and grammatically improper as I Liberate me from me so read My Wisdom Breathes out loud and

Read My Wisdom Breathes as you wrote the book allow the book to raise you out of your thinking knowing memory mind as My Wisdom Breathes is written to stop you from romancing your past and

Quit creating stories to make your past nostalgic discharging your offended emotions and slighted feelings opening the way for you to soar out of your past to live and experience a nunow nirvana

My Wisdom Breathes is a book written to be carried with you wherever you go and when you are experiencing a bad day you can open My Wisdom Breathes to any page and expand out of your bad day

To exhilarate optimistic spunk that accelerates innovative agility that rousts out rebellious resolve to evolve of enterprising vigor feeling your intestinal fortitude feel alive like a beehive sensing freedom

As I wrote My Wisdom Breathes to show people the way I expanded my life to open your eyes to glide through life with listeners inspirations awakened your entertainers fame to flow through you

As My Wisdom Breathes expands you out of yesterday to energize today to enterprise your dreams to experience your life of lavish leisure basking of sun of the fun splendor now and forever more

Glossary for New Words
Yazz/Yazza ultrapowerful

The **limbic system** is a set of structures in the brain that deal with emotions and memory fight flight or freeze

Aggrandizing: To widen in scope increase in size or intensity enlarge extend

Beau Sabreur: A handsome adventurer

Bodhi: Supreme enlightenment

Bravado: Vaunted display of courage or self-confidence or swagger

Chronicled: a chronological record of events; a history

Crapeyetice: having shitty outlook about life

Chronicled Minds: the unconscious and subconscious minds

Recorded Minds: the unconscious and subconscious minds

Submerged Minds: the unconscious and subconscious minds

Éclat: Brilliance of success, reputation

Esprit: Sprightliness of spirit or wit or lively brainpower

Herdocracy: Trying to fit in with the in crowd and following societies ways

Inlightenmint: Sweet illuminated awakening to my intimate imaginative artistry

IIWIIITT: Illuminated Imagination wisdom inspiration intuition innovation trailblazer talent

Innerprising: Imaginative colorful nirvana neon's every day rapturous intuitive savvy invigorating nunow gumptions to expand your dreams

Kevalin: One who is set free from matter: a liberated soul

Noo: Numinous outlaw optimism

Numen: Divine Spirit or Power

Nous: Shrewdness understanding or savvy

Nouvelle Vague: A new wave, trend)

Nunow: Ultrabright Present Moment

Nowbirthed: Present moment innovations

Nowborn: Imagination birthed in this moment

Nowfangled: Ultra fresh fashioned scenarios

Outré: Passing the boundaries of what I currently know and think

Perspicacious: Having the power of seeing clearly; quick-sighted; sharp of sight

Prescience: (presh-*uh*ns) knowledge of things before they exist or happen; foreknowledge; foresight.

Pansophy: Universal Wisdom

Quiteyetice: (quit-eye-tice) Caving into the past with a low self-esteem quitting at the first uncomfortable event

Requiescence: A state of rest or repose; peace, quiet.

Savoir-Faire: Insight of just what to do in any situation; tact

Tabula Rasa: An opportunity for a fresh start or clean slate

Thaumaturgy: Worker of Miracles

Twiteyetice: My bogus inner ridicule

Turdocracy: Following people stepping in their BS

Secret Society: People that manipulate the world affairs

Societyeyetice: Stuck in political correctness

Victimeyetice: Bellyaching about everything

Wininity: Wisdom invigorates nowborn innovative nirvana instigating trailblazer yazzapizzazz

Yazzajazzes: Dancing with day to day celebrations

Yazzapizzazz: My charismatic charm expanding me through life

Yazzapanache: ultrapowerful stylish flair exuding animated verve showcasing globetrotter talent

Yazzasnazzy: Colorful entertaining outcome

The Map

I now fathom and esteem my map is never my terra incognita as my
terra incognita is my unexampled and unexplored wilderness that
stylishly exhibits my divine treasured abundances revering rapturous

Animated imaginative nirvana celebrating omnificence galvanizes
nowbirthed innovative torchbearer audacity that strolled me out of
my implanted map onto my terra incognita Tropical Paradises

That excited my trailblazer curiosity that energized my pioneering
ingenuity that initiated my clairvoyant intuition that stimulated
my enterprising éclat savvy electrifying my wanders will to see

My cosmos as my panorama splendor opened my listening eyes
and seeing ears to witness my universe as my everlasting bliss that
forever kissed me with my breathtaking grandeur today and every

Day in every way I smile of gratitude exhibiting my grin of
appreciation that awakened me to understand and concede I was
unknowingly controlled by my imbedded map that I naively instilled

From history media manipulation school system my parents circle
of influence ancestor's society and the arrogant leaders of the world
that I followed and taught myself to mimic my daily life after

The above-named tutors and metaphors that entrenched my
yesterdays because that is what everybody else did trying to
hide inside society's ways as my self-taught factoids are

Something resembling a fact that is unverified and often fabricated
data that ingrained my map fears and scaredy cat bratiness along
with the emotional trauma dramatized feelings and as I heard

The protagonist exaggerations pertaining to that event as the onlookers spewed their factoids to make themselves feel important about themselves as I now realize and admit the graphic and verbal

Versions from their input and my inner reactions shaped my subconscious and unconscious characterizations good bad or uncaring implemented who knows what is in my recorded settings

As I now grasp and concede dramatized traumatized and exaggerated events insert hidden restrictions create uneasy emotions and underlying fears I installed from my childhood encounters parent's

Ancestor's the way people lived their life and handled their daily encounters as I experienced my day to day life is the way I taught myself and the way I ingrained my map and my map is everything

I think and know are yesterday's memories views opinions and beliefs were embedded from birth till now from the socialized systems of what other people wanted me to know and standards

They wanted me to live by today all went away yesterday as I now understand and admire my map is never my terra incognita Promised Land of Grand to understand and esteem my map is formatted

Illustrations that trigger the snapshots that have similar illustrations so every time I encounter a similar event or person activates that representation that actuates my first reactions

That are quickly initiated within my subconscious scenery as I ask. What hides in the stealth recordings and representations in our subconscious and unconscious that we are clueless about?

That is created by my endless links to my past as I ask. How has my mind maps controlled and subdued me into yesterday? As I now realize and admit I will forever think know and remember my way to

All my yesterday's that awakened my pioneering spirit rousted out my
cowboy up gumption to saddle up my mountain bred mustang to ride
hell bent for election out of yesterday to easily lope straight onto

My divine paradises as I am excitedly exploring my uncharted
treasures of my terra incognita vast rivers of riches that minted
my mystical spontaneity neon's my trails of triumph cleared

Away my trying to change heal create transform and using forgiveness
that allowed my map to unknowingly control my life kept me
forever stifled in memory as I dispelled and melted the words

Mind change heal create transformation forgiveness blame shame
and attached charged up memory's bitter feelings sour emotions
and unsavory representations from my day to day life and lingo

I instantly discovered and conceded my minds are filled with recorded
ambiguity that channeled the way I think and know trying to
change heal create transform and utilizing forgiveness to change

My life only to realize and concede change activates annoyed emotions
agonizing feelings and unsavory thoughts as forgiveness never
discharges the event forgiveness is feel good yet never liberation

Appreciation is liberation the more I tried to change heal create and
transform my life the more I kept repeating the same antiquated
thoughts and moving the furniture around throughout my inner

Landscape staying the same rerunning incapacitating sarcasm trying
to change my thinking and knowing then trying to create and
transform my life from my mapped opinions and beliefs that are now

Extinct and gone from my life as instantly awakened my adventurous
acuity that electrified my warrior gumption to the liberating power of
understand expand energize enterprise experience and appreciation

That discharged and disconnected my wounded emotions hurt feelings
turned down the volume making the past greyed out to be featureless
blameless and depersonalized making my past a previous world

Liberated me to be instantly introduced to my futuristic fashion
designer that turned up the neon color and vibrant volume on my
nunow wow embellishes my walk of wisdom celebrations exhilarates

My will to thrill me to feel healthy wealth and wise as I understand
and admire the audacious power of expand energize enterprise
experience appreciation and celebration because these lyrics are

Now my classy artistic lexicons of fond that electrify my pathfinder
foresight and maverick tenacity as I now express and utilize the
wizardry of expand over change energize over transformation

As I desire to power up my dreams and turn on my desired life as
I express to all people utilize the acuity of enterprise over create
because trying create I'm baffled in my yesterday's think and know

As I enterprise I surprise myself with awakened farseeing feelings
energetic emotions and tabula rasa revelations excite my innerprising
innovations and appreciation of over forgiveness as my spirited

Passions sketched my tabula rasa exposés and visionary cognizance
are alive and thriving traveling through my terra incognita paradises
as I appreciate the event I intentionally received the life expanding

Insight from that event energized my selfworth and dethroned the
heartache swiftly disbanded the torment of that event as I dissolved
and eliminated the word mind to utilizing celebrations raised

My inlightened vibrations of self-esteem relishing of my accomplished
outcomes illuminates my core decor as I dethroned think know
thoughts memory and mind from my life to understand and esteem

Innovation dissolves thinking as understanding disentangles knowing
energizing my wisdom opened trailblazer curiosity that canonizes
unexampled revolutionary intrepid optimism stimulates trailbreaker

Yazzapizzazz as inspiration disconnects timid thoughts and me from
yesterday as I now realize and admire my map contains everything
I recorded from yesterday as my terra incognita is my stylish

Today's enterprising feelings revolutionary emotions rapturous
animated imaginative nibbana celebrations optimizing gleeful nunow
ingenious trendsetting acumen to dance me through life feeling

My detached panache that enhances my basking on my beaches
of breathtaking felicity now and forever more I soar of trailblazer
curiosity trusting my frontiersman lore as I fathom and admire

My Life of Riley feeling luminous luck as I AM basking in my
vacationers' paradises strolling on my seashores of stunning serenity
as I feel my fiery foresight energized my holidaymaker gumption

My Wisdom Breathes

I feel my wisdom breathes imaginative inlightenmint sweetening
my dreams to be my every day unconventional lifestyle as I
float of frontiersman lore optimizing autonomous temerity

That married my spiritual physical and eternal extravaganzas
of stunning utopia magically brightens ingenious wizardry
to flow through my stylist savoir-faire flair painting

My inner scenery with my breaths of regal rainbow vibrancy
aggrandizing today's heavenly extravaganzas shines my
divine *wininity as I now fathom and admire

My wisdom breathes frequencies of futuristic revelations electrifying
quick-witted ultra-bright numinous celebrations instigated enterprising
splendor to be my way of stylishly loving life as I unleash

My bold rabble-rousing enthusiasm exhilarates adventurous
trendsetter hutzpah energizing outré nouvelle vague tabula
rasa mystique matures unique quixotic nirvana

As I dance with my life's venturous moneymaker nous that
excites my nowfangled felicity that instantly unlocked my
revolutionary optimist ubiquitous supernatural savvy

To flow through veins of fame swiftly opened my daily abundant
ventures so I deliberately flow of my received moneyed up
accomplishmints witnessing my sweet neat success I appreciate

As I expand people's innovative wit to experience their dreams
as I fleetingly understand and admire my wisdom breathes
peerless utopian acuity uncoupling my unconscious anchors

Instantly stopped me from doing what I have always done that
was me baking the cake of bellyaching crap frosting the cake with
cantankerous BS created my dawdling bitching wallowing

In subconscious blame and shame that crossed out of my life
today instantly opening my prospering pathways of my canny
curiosity uncovering and discovering my unexampled talent

To expand through life as I swiftly inhaled inspiration as I eloquently
articulated my wisdom breathes rainbow brilliance coloring the world
with my canny charismatic charm gleams my ingenious affluent

Northern light luminosity electrifying the earth's airwaves with my
warm radiant grandeur as I now understand my wisdom breathes
my nunow wow clarifies my wisdom optimizes wealth because

Wisdom confuses my thinking mind opening my unconscious curiosity
deftly expands me out of my hidden ancestral anchors that created my
thoughts of anxiety that riled up my survival thinking that stressed

Me out in doubt that left me yesterday energizing my canonized clout
animates my wisdom breathes my candid acuity that I can never be
negative about anything as I am witnessing hearing and adhering to

My imagination that energized my lionized optimistic insight as I now
esteem and realize my acumen ascends my daredevil tenacity exhales
my liberating vigor ousting all my outside oppressors emancipating

Me from me in an appreciative flash applauding and energizing my
gladiator gumption that senses my exalting emotions autonomous
agilities to forthrightly feel typhoons of triumph to expand

People and the world out of their survival mode rhetoric because
my wisdom breathes eager snooping skills that thrill my sovereign
audacity to instantly discharge and dissolve my subconscious

Programming opening my farsighted clairvoyance to entrust my
listening eyes and seeing ears to witness my keen felicity and feel
my copious cornucopia that I deliberately chosen to receive from

Everywhere in a funloving flair as I intentionally appreciate my
spirit dares that are my life expanding awards or challenges as
I now realize and esteem my challenges are domestic jokers

That instantly energize my straightforward spunk as my wisdom
breathes my manifesting magnetism that charms the universe's
frequencies of easy street living purposefully awakens

Me in a cool natural way as I now understand and admire money is
an energy of my innovative prowess and dexterity that intentionally
magnifies the cosmic airwaves with my heartfelt thank you

To instantly manifest my Shangri La pageantry in a calm balmy
serene way as I play today my way that lights up my spontaneous
shrewdness that instantly jumpstarted my conscious celebrations

Ceremoniously escalated my legendary lore electrifying my brilliant
reveries aggrandizes my torchbearers' inquisitive omniscient
omnificence that ennobles my stupendous inventors' wit

That rocketed me onward and upward feeling energized let's fly
visionary passions of my enterprising magical mystique unleashed my
trailblazer imagination optimizing nowborn ambitions explicitly

Awakened me to understand and admire to expand through and
out of yesterday I inhale artistic visions as my wisdom breathes my
noble magnificence quickly glorifies my head honcho celebrations

As I purposely received my lavish endless abundances in a gigantic
daring upbeat way as my inlightened eyes open my nirvana ears
purified my cosmic airwaves of excellent health and wealth

To smell my hellacious luxurious fragrances of my financial freedom
as I touched the silk splendor of victory as I audaciously feel the
serenity of being rebelliously alive and thriving of sightseer

Innocence animates my moviemaker inspirations let's fly my wisdom
breathes my imaginative imagery energizes my intuitive wizardry
that awakened my pioneering legacies that clearly stream through

The universe as I now grasp and respect my wisdom breathes
rad gladden outré omnificence as I pass the boundaries of myself
taught stuff and unconscious anchors as I instantly unsheathed

My troublemaker tenacity that awakened my enterprising desires
unwavering trust and lionhearted dignity of my unexampled
inventors' skills thrilled my torchbearer curiosity powered on

My visionary optimism lionized ardor articulation that excited my
space-age fashion designer parading my Picasso Prowess that dawns
immaculate spectaculars illuminating my breathtaking picturesque

Imagery turned on my trailblazing tabula rasa inspirations that
excited my nouvelle vague enthusiasm gleams my new waves of
wondrous imagination opening my intrinsic leadership integrity

That outlined designed drew colored and painted my venturesome
visualizations on my third eye movie screen that powered up
my pristine brainpower and panorama brainprowess colored

My uncharted featureless frontiers in neon nirvana as my prime-
time modernizer and angelic artistry energized and enterprized my
futuristic foresight and my dreams imagery pristinely decorated

My peaceful prosperous animated luxury on my earthly horizons as
my cognizant scenery and on all the horizons in my daily life are mural
of my dreams as my wisdom breathes risk-taking avant-garde spunk

Of my imaginative supernatural mystique maturing my enterprising
entrepreneurial skills thrilling my ride and rope resolve as I
AM energized and wise waltzing internally spry energizing

I AM healthy wealthy and wonderfully escalating my jovial
jubilees of sovereignty that stroll me onto my boulevards of
beautiful cosmic extravaganzas as I now esteem and gleam

My supernatural insight breathes my colorful charm disarms
the world's negativity with nowborn enthusiastic gumption
ascending trendsetter designers' vibrant innovative treasures

Yessing I AM blessed gleaming my rainbow splendor
through the earth's airwaves awakening my venturous
bravery within me and all people as we all dance

At our bountiful ball of beautiful bliss kissing the universe
with our empathy now and forever more I soar as my wisdom
breathes my prestigious integrity and plush lush love to all

Wakeup Noo

I now wake up noo (new) naturally optimistic optimizing synergy
titillates my enterprising wizardry everyday as I now understand and
the power of waking noo whooshes my venturesome numinous

Outlaw omnificence let's fly my terrific trendsetter tenacity
witnessing my sunrise praises of peace on earth energizes my
miraculous mornings cheerfully opening my heart eyes to see

My wonderful world of stunning splendor with wisdom beaming
brightly into my listening eyes that unleashes my soul's visionary vigor
unleashes my trailblazer valor authorizes me stroll through life with

My luminary inspirational foresight enthuses my mystical
endeavoring muse to light my fuse of futuristic utopian savvy
exalting my frontiersman fortitude to ride through my life as

The mountain men leaving St Louis Missouri in the early 1800's as
I now realize and admire today I AM the mountain man leaving St.
Louis to venture through my terra incognita mountain ranges of

My dreams that cleared the way for me to wake noo with wanders
animated kevalin elucidated nowbirthed organismic out of this world
insight as I stroll through life I feel my gallant valor of adventure

Electrifies my courageous clairvoyance canny curiosity and spine-
tingling savvy electrifies my moneyed up dreams with swashbuckler
sass to be biggest boldest brightest vibrant oasis of my life

Thrilled my trailbreaker lore spurred my nowborn mountaineer
farsighted enthusiasm inspired my trailblazer audacity and unwavering
resiliency entrusting my imagination wisdom inspiration intuition

Innovation sixth sense prescience and trailblazer talent to confidently
and clairvoyantly understand my trails before me to soar of stunning
well-heeled riches as I now wakeup noo with hellraiser woo

To get on with my day of fun of the sun splendor because I left all
my rat a tat crap from yesterday and before in my rearview mirror as
stupendously witness my colorful clear blue skies of wise energizing

My nowbrithed classy sovereign selfworth to understand and
admire my fire of desire within me to dance extravagantly successful
intimately streams my happy-go-lucky shrewdness to experience

My nowography nirvana with troublemaker wit as I briskly strutted
down my trails of tranquility to sit in rocking chair of robust riches as
I stopped bitching and bellyaching about stuff that has/had zero effect

On my life unless I give it energy good bad or indifferent as I grasp
and esteem I can only bitch and bellyache about yesterday or before
so now I leave yesterday and before snoring as I daringly prodded

My wanders mettle kinetically enthused my pathfinder poise
because I left trying to be perfect in yesterday dawning my nowborn
bravura as I AM hellaciously healthy wealthy and astute

Now and forever more fathoming and esteeming my more
soars my idealists' revelations electrifying my spiritual sanguine
savvy cleared my ingenious eyes to hear see and trust

My forerunner felicity that excites my wanders whimsical will to
feel hear see taste and touch ultramodern utopia awakening my
Presidential Preeminence jetting my bold Commander-in Chief

Pacesetter-wit as I am skywriting I AM awe-inspiring awesome
innovating audacious action with my sassy mountaineer flair
entices my rabble-rousing innovative trailblazer tenacity

To understand and admit my poverty consciousness had me to jealous and envious of successful people as I walked thru my day to day life with lewd larcenists' words and thoughts stealing

My dreams via my poverty conscious pity me habits and excuse ridden behaviors too afraid of adversity and controversy to succeed because I now fathom and esteem adversity and

Controversy unweave my virtuous versatility to walk on my Broadway of copious cornucopia because I blatantly pulled out all my needy weedy crappy conniving ways of despising

Myself because bitching and bellyaching was me despising myself and my abilities was left in St. Louis yesteryear as I now realize and witness throughout the world people stay poor because

Of societized system of lack then talking about what other people have and complaining about what they lack so bellyachers and complainers stay stuck in poverty as people talk

About poverty then stewing on their poo of never do rather than saying I began back when realizing and stating I won here and now as I grasp and state here and now I AM crowned

The winner of my dreams bright now as I travel through limbo to embrace my rich Garden of Eden yet I realize my current life and present knowledge are naïve to the path

Across my life escalating limbo as my omnific oomph stops me from hearing my knowing thinking memory mind and people that are in same place disgusted speaking and thinking in dislike

As I ask When I speak and think about poverty how can anything new arrive in my life? Opens me up to realize when I bitch about my life I feel poverty and insecurity that lets fly

ROBERT A. WILSON

My entrepreneurial spirit question How does thoughts about other
people's chattels with envy stop me? How do I fail when I look
for somebody else to expand my life? It stops me and flatly

Created my bitching and bellyaching fetches my memories
of poverty conscious looking for somebody keeps me on my
dreadmill Why does the same thing keep happening to me?

As my noo fathoms and esteem wise outside sources give me
wisdom and unexplainable agility that expands me out yesterday
to my new frontiers of financial freedom as I realize and admit

To give something to somebody for free never does anything
for them or me as I now realize and admit I have given people
books and stuff for free and they do zero with them

As I now realize and esteem giving people something for zilch
creates a mental they will be back tomorrow wanting more
for zilch as I now admit and value giving something

For zilch get both parties zilch as I wake up noo my nervy
omniscience is omnipresent to expand energize and enterprise
this day with daredevil acumen yazzapizzazzes

My jazzy razzle-dazzle enthusiasm excited my wakeup noo
feeling nirvana opulence ornate's my innate potentate prowess
thrusting me upward and onward stop looking over there

Swiftly opened my laser eyes and seers' ears to grasp and
admire my daily life shows me the way to peaceful prosperous
Garden of Eden as my listening enthusiast hearkens

My ultra-unique imaginative imagery wanders wisdom inaudible
inspirations magical intuition unleashing my innovative talents
to ballet me through my day to day life mirrors a trapeze

Artist swinging from swing to swing because I now realize and admit my spirited grit get and go sashays me defiantly up my trails of realization polished my wakeup noo numinous out

This world optimism lets fly my intuitive spiritual mystique within me as I feel my unique universe unleash my nowbirthed imaginative visionary epiphanies revolutionizing

Spectacular entrepreneurial thrillpower tantalizes hellraisers resolve invigorating luminous lore powered up omnific wisdom and enterprising gumption as I instantly celebrate rapturous

Amazing peace within me as I AM Free of me to enjoy elegant tranquility salsa my life with stunning success because I am blessed now and forever more I soar of spiritual poise feeling

My wakeup noo whooshes in my nomad I AM Glad I AM classy sassy sovereign with me experiencing my sprees of copious ecstasy seeing my life through rose colored glasses

Lightning Bolt Clarity

I feel my lightning bolt clarity crack the whip of my thrillpower
temerity igniting my canny rebellious acumen canonizing kevalin
inlightenmint sweetening my selfworth to expand me out

Of my gloom and doom slogs of self-misery instantly stimulating
my boom and bloom bravado (vaunted display of courage or
self-confidence; swagger) astutely shredding and deleting

My blemished mindsets shameful reactions all subconscious and
unconscious dreads so I instantly tossed my heckling anxieties in
the gutter too hurry and scurry out of my life now this liberating

Performance suddenly dawned my robust entrusting autonomous
idealists savvy letting fly my indigenous ingenuity that inspirationally
excites my groundbreaking pansophy (universal wisdom)

That enthuses my artistic dexterity to mature strengthen and
emprise's my venturous virtuosity to experience my pure ritzy glitzy
gusto as I feel honoured that I encompassed the guts to unravel

My inner hidden gunk that funked up my life to instantly galvanizing
my unexampled sassy trendsetter optimist lore to understand
and admire my life is forever a mystical magical miraculous

Mystery streaming my classy canny nous clears innerprising curiosity
to masterfully admire my life flow and glows of ingenious riddles
that snapped cracked and popped my lightning bold clarity

That instantly burst open my visionary imagery rousted out
my trailboss omniscience to ride my trails of turmoil with
a keen clairvoyance trusting my gladiator gumption

To appreciate my amazing gifted triumphs as I appreciatively
bask on my mountain tops of majestic tranquility overlooking my
oceans of magnificence surfing my seas of marvelous success

As I am blessed with lightning bolt clarity and purified
groundbreaking prowess to wow me with my nowborn nirvana as
I now witnessed and felt my lightning bolt clarity snapped me

Out of yesterday to be of my nunow wow to waltz of windfalls of
wealth that energized my stroll of serenity tantalizing resplendent
glorious leisure lighting up my seas of beautiful blessings

Today and every day in every way appreciating my regal majesty
inspired my animated ardor soars of clairvoyant elucidation that
lumens my ultrabright dreamers dazzling imagery entices

My moviemaker magic that initiated my high-spirited wit to understand
and admire that adversity and controversy showed me my paths to
my royal paradises as I now masterfully understand every encounter

I receive a unique enterprising life achievement award for me
to masterfully admire as my peerless present moment gifts that
expanded beyond my existing thinking knowing memory mind

That dethroned my attached reactions indignant mindset big-headed
pride know it all illiteracy worn out opinion's bane viewpoints
my ancestors' voiceless fallacies hiding in the bushes around

Every corner controlled my thinking entrenched my rat a tat rhetoric
that controlled me internally and externally is gone like yesterday's
dawn as I'm aware in that moment in time that was the way

Our ancestors survived along with the untamed landscape
the indigenous wisdom language barriers having to learn new
communication abilities along with the way as I ask

How do people today lack communication skills to expand out
of the same challenges as our ancestors? I expanded out this
question because I realized and conceded I embodied similar

Low-quality communication skills by admitted and shucking this stuff I
AM rewarded with my Life of Riley from my courage and confidence to
expand trusting my optimistic fortitude that thrilled my lightning bolt

Clarity canonized my listeners enthusiast brilliance purifying
my communicators rapport clarified my potentate prowess that
wowed my wondrous oracle wisdom rainbowed brilliant

Colorful omnipotent risk-taking yazzapanache that parties me through
life with a detached daredevilry electrifying my sovereign audacity
to admit I tried to think and know my way through life perished

Now as I awakened to grasp and admire my unique epiphanies are
my nunow wow optimized my guru spirit and poetic poise robustly
rouse from deep within me masterfully echoed my lightning bolt

Clarity cracked my whip of whizz bang wisdom as I now realize
and admire negativity is my self-ingrained history that created my
thinking knowing and memories living my current life through

Yesterday's effigies of gee whiz what is going on with me because I
changed my thinking yet my life is still that same mundane insanity
by understand and admitting this to me myself and I as let fly

My fancy flight of inlightened numen nerve elegantly grinning happy-
go-lucky vibes liberates my ingenious vitality intuits trendsetter
yazzagumption to saddle up my pathfinder prowess to clear away

My selfish debris of yesterday opening a path of prestigious
affluence today harmonizing my spiritual wise trusting my
supernatural clairvoyance and day to day inlightened insight

To tranquilly stroll through life because my negativity is gone bonding
me with my nunow enterprising gumption actuating thaumaturgy
ingenuity envisioned my ingenious triumphs yazzajazzes

My head honcho hutzpah to understand and esteem I expanded out of
my crabby pessimism to expand of my nowborn nirvana sophistication
that galvanized my audacious trailboss dexterity vigorously

Initiating unwavering trust to flow through my arteries of artistic bliss
elucidated my innate imaginative luxury stimulated my intrinsic verve
unlatched my dashing panache unfetters dreamers' legacies spawns

My pert dignity that intimately vanguards my stylish vacationers
yazzapizzazz that chimes the rhymes of my prime-time sublime divine
wininity that flashed my dazzling lightning bolt clarity energized

My laser bright insight let's fly fervor perky adroit acuity instantly
liberated my inborn gumption heralds my torchbearer charm
to disarmed my worrywart retorts that caused me to react

With neurotic nullifying narcissism directly created my corruptible
crass as I now grasp and concede I acted like an arrogant ass rejecting
everybody's input unlocked my courage to grasp and admit

All my self-spoken sarcasm created my timid thoughts and my
guarded thinking I was never good or smart enough I heard from my
mumbled sarcasm then hearing matching words from outer sources

Then I would smugly buck up and reject fresh wisdom then I would
timidly cover up fears with smart ass retorts concealing I lacked
the wisdom to understand what was being spoken trying to look

Cool externally yet internally I shutdown with scaredy cat groveling
as I buried my insulted emotions offended feelings deep within me
as I built a wall of pity me paradoxes as I would creep away from

Anything that pushed that timid limits As I now understand and admit
from in the womb thru toddler thru adolescence high school till today
those attached emotions and hurt feelings control me until now

As I opened up hear and grasp the wisdom that was being spoken so I
liberated me from my childhood to experience my dreams pronto as I
let fly my high-tech imagination intensified my confidence clarified

My spine-tingling savvy amplifies my fashion designer talent
unsheathed lightning bolt clarity energized my laser beam esteemed
enterprising sassy tenacity animated my moneymaker resolve

To understand and admire my nowborn bravura revolutioneyeszed
adroit vigor unlocked robust autonomous trust tantalizing
my vanguard vibrancy to understand and admire...

I AM the visionary leader gleaming lightning bolt clarity
celebrating life's affluent riches invigorating treasures yazzes my
life of lavish luxurious leisure now and forever more I fly

Dissolving Excuses

I asked me. How does blaming outside sources for my current situation create my victimizing excuses that pilfered my inner peace then are the thieves of my dreams? This question unlocked

My wise morality to grasp and admit I bitch and complain my way to the outhouse as I instigate my innate valorous prowess that strolls me onto the elevator that glides my up to my lush penthouse

Celebrations experiencing serene peace and plush prosperity as I rousted out my backbone integrity spine tingling sovereignty to stop bitching and complaining about my parents' my profession and

Current events because I now admit and grasp my parents my occupation or anyone person or persons has/had zilch to do with my current way of life today because I created my current life thru

Being know it all unwilling to listen and my arrogant ignorance shut me down internally built my prison of shame that imprisoned me with insecurity and immaturity that locked me away from my skills

As I created my encyclopedia of excuses that hooked me into yesterday as I now realize and concede blaming my parents' my chosen profession and everything that went wrong was

Somebody else's doing was my everlasting glue of never do because I was afraid to admit and grasp I lacked internal valor to rise above my challenges I was afraid of my gifts because of my self-teachings and

Inner preaching's about everything I thought I lacked was my fake and bake quackery so I decisively sacked the quakes sent them packing to extinction distinctly ignited my warrior courage confidence

Spiritual maturity and the savvy skills to receive and appreciate
my life events escalates my éclat [brilliance of success] elucidation
as I now awakened to innovatively respect everything

That goes awry is to energetically open my wise eyes to see my
present moment gifts gleams my immaculate thank you to the
world and all people as now is the time the time to get off

My couch of grouch that created my chronic ouch bitching about my
day to day life stained my brain and inner backdrops with silly shams
of damn that I told myself I was never going to fail without grasping

I fail my way to success then I fell prey to my boneheaded bratty BS
that kept me in the dark farces of my crabby clumsy thinking that
the outside world had everything to do with me and dreams was

My despondent illusions governing my life as I was being a puppet as I
asked me… How did I or how do I create excuses that keep me stuck in
life blaming others and feeling shameful emotions control me today?

That was my thinking stinking up my inner structures as I cleared
away my innermost debris to free me myself and I to understand
and concede I know in blame and think in shame afraid

Of my dreams because my dreams are inside me to be expressed to
my physical world through my will to expand out of yesterday as I
now understand and admit I allowed my outside world control

Me because I thought I change my physical world all would be
well and when that failed to occur I fell prey to my pity me palaver
as I excused me myself and I from my dreams and desired life

By using excuses that it was my parents fault my mom or dad did this
to me or somebody did this to me I thought and my environment in
which I lived was my problem as I now understand and concede

I existed in a life filled with excuses riddled with fear that stifled me
in delusional emotional deception thinking my external world controls
my life which is a fallacy of fraudulent ignorance that kept my lies

Of putrid pity me victimitice crapitice that kept me weeping in wimpy
status quo whoa and stuck in couch potatoeyetice being the couch
grouch blaming others for my life situation feeling sabotaging sorry

For myself with discouraging emotions belching welching complaining
creating dream stealing despair thinking life is never fair Why is this
happening to me? That instilled my peevish paralyzing palaver and

Worrywart thinking as I now brashly tell all my internal external and
eternal naysayers to go enjoy their private fires of hell as I hand them
all a personalized map telling them to take their rat a tat crap and

Go away in a loving way as I now awakened to hear and adhere to my
fiery foresight dissolved my thinking in hindsight looking back thoughts
because hindsight is looking back as foresight is looking forward with

Intestinal fortitude understanding wisdom and inspiration of my
present moment events clear my wise eyes and open seers' ears to
witness my Life of Riley as I unsealed my inventors yazzapanache

Let's fly my sassy classy sex appeal beams my zestful zeal thru
the universe as I instantly realize and admit history is something
somebody else wants me to know and learn as the silent society is

The author of our history books that slyly controls the world today
so How is the world stuck in history? How does that question expose
history as tory to the people and the sly control of the secret society?

As I rousted out my rabble-rousing resolve to understand and admit
everything in the school curriculums and school systems is something
somebody else wants me and other people to know learn and

ROBERT A. WILSON

Remember to control our life's through unconscious programming and
conscious thinking as I now admit and understand history is a learned
pattern of yesterday unconscious habits and haunts of the stealthy

Societies domination as I now realize and admit I can control any
country by controlling the currency writing and publishing the
books the school systems uses from preschool to the college to

Silently control the country as I now feel my unbound yazzapizzazz
flow thru my autonomous arteries liberating me from my self-taught
annoyances energizes my canonized creeds to admit and fathom

I made or make up excuses to sooth my egotistical arrogance and
know it all ignorance to cover up mistakes stopped long ago as I now
stand up with responsibility with shoulders back accountability

Embracing my perky inspiration that empowers me to expand out
of retaliatory malice because since the beginning of time eye for an
eye retaliatory spite has been the way of the world as I tried settle

Differences through tyrant rants of rage that engaged my subconscious
angry programming that allowed my external events and people
to control my life all passed away today as I shit canned

My lewd angry lunacy to uncover and discover my hellraisers heart
and thrillpower soul that disarmed my inner harming haunts that
lurk like jerks inside me always waited and baited me into turmoil

So I stopped caving into my external settings to instantly grasp and
admire I AM the leader of my life innerprising my inner scenery feeling
calm canny dignity as I instantly awaken to understand and esteem

I innovated my current situation good bad or indifferent as I expand
energize and enterprise my inborn scenarios sensing my stunning
splendor flow thru my hellraiser heart and pristine soul cherishing

I AM accountable to my core values to expand my wealth and success with my billionaire talents I lit up my internal fervor epiphanies graben my saddle horn of life swinging aboard my galloping mustang

Of my glorious adventures lionizing lionhearted optimism just boldly kicking all the life sapping crap out of my life now and forever to instantly thrive of intimate serenity sheens vibrant numinous ecstasy

That eases me through my day to day experiences as I now understand and esteem I encompass he courage confidence wisdom inspiration and campaigner's talent to express the truth about

My life events as I expand my grandeur geysers my sunrise praises of peace that manifests my life of luxurious leisure as I experience basking of my sun of fun fervor utopia nirvana that streams thru me

Myself and I steam heats my frontiersman blood lighting up my frontier scenery enterprising my futuristic foresight endearing me to my visionary vitality now and forever more I soar of spiritual valor

Deathless Wisdom

I now feel and admire my deathless wisdom dawns eternal awakenings
titivates luminous enlightenmint stimulating stupendous wizardry
enlivens my dreamers magic and out of this world wisdom

That appears from everywhere enthusiastically streams through all
phases of my amazing life sweetens my dreams instantly as I now express
my newfangled inspired fiery intuition that strolls me effortlessly onto

My trails of triumph illuminated my numinous lore that gleams
my zestful legacies electrifying animated mystical savvy that steam
heats my hellraisers crazy enterprising omnificence yazzajazzes

My optimist's dexterity unleashes my marvelous charming celebrations
as I travel on my pristine mountain passes relishing the scenic peace and
stunning splendor as I fostered my kingdoms of stylish extravagance

By traveling my routes of tribulation chopping down my widow maker
(detached or broken limb or tree top) challenges so I now feel my
innovative emotions energize my wanders will to fathom and esteem

My deathless wisdom saunters me through life with enthused maverick
mystique to feel alive with venturer's verve illuminates my magical flair
as I recognize and admire I wave my magic wand of acuity instantly

Ascends my noble daredevilry frees me to understand and
esteem I AM the mystical magical miracle of my life with
my core celestial festivities lighting up my trailblazer's
temerity energizing my self-assured audacity trusting

My backbone brilliance sassily strolls me through life with greatest of
ease as I awaken to discharge and dissolve my jealousy envy and all
pessimistic thoughts about other people my work environment and

Daily life authorized me to admit and disconnect my being jealous
envious discharging my cynical rat a tat rhetoric about myself and
other people that were on my life path my daily encounters work

Environment and people in management positions as I would
arrogantly tell others all the ways I could do better was my head
up my butt burping BS stressing me out in doubt pouting about

Everything left me yesterday as I avow I AM free as a cloud floating
through the air on warm summers day as I instantly rocketed away
on my rocket ship of lavish luxurious bliss and humble heavenly

Gratitude unleashing my voyager's appreciation I let fly my life force
I deliberately dethroned and detached my seedy weedy greediness
instantly blessed me to experience my dreamers' paradises mirrors

Walking out of cave into Disney Land energized my flight of fancy
foresight exhilarated my sun lit grit get and go to stroll up my trails of
triumph that let fly my grinning gumption trusting my trailblazer

Temerity realizing and admitting to expand my life I cut the ties
to my egotistical arrogance know it all ignorance and my ancestors
voiceless grip on my life today as I now beam my dazzling debonair

Flair feeling loved appreciating internal robust trust of my ability's
agility imagination wisdom inspiration and innovative talent
to ride through life trusting my listening enthusiast and

My troublemaker trendsetter simplicity to understand and
admire I AM a dexterous globetrotter effortlessly enterprising and
escalating my clever fortes and animated vigor saunters me thru

My dreamer's confusion because confusion is raw wisdom celebrating
exhilarating nibbana felicity unleashing stupendous ingenious swing
for the fence's brilliancy as I entrusted my esteemed deathless

Wisdom to hit my home run of fun that tangos with my effervescent
agility turned on my hellacious VIP sapience spicing up my audacious
potentate inlightenmint energized my sweet numinous galas that stirred

My forthright fury to appreciate my quick-witted pizzazz
and risk taker flair elucidates my innate unworldly stamina
actuates dazzling health and wealth electrifies my whirlwinds
of inspiration daylights optimist's omnipotence

As I now realize and value my wisdom is beyond my knowing zone as
I now understand and concede I think inside what I know bequeaths
me to whatever is familiar comfortable and everything I have done

To this point yet I want to live my life of Riley and never ever having
to let go of anything as I now realize and admit my knowing zone is
my memory mind anchored in yesterday because my past is what it is

Good bad or indifferent is the root of my thinking knowing and
memories that controls the way I interact within myself transfers that to
my physical world as I admit I was stuck inside whatever I taught myself

As I now admit and grasp my outside influences were the programmers
of what I taught myself so quickly I unshackled my innermost worrywart
hecklers as I admit and value I am responsible and accountable for

everything I taught myself to realizing and admiring my deathless
wisdom dawns eternal acuity titillating hellraisers lore elates sovereign
savvy wondrously invigorates my dreamer's optimism mystically clears

My avenues of awesome grandeur as I stroll upon my classy everlasting
charismatic charm that glistens through the stratosphere as I now fathom
and esteem my visionary spontaneity is my clever canny mysteries

Intentionally confusing me to investigate my inner clairvoyant
inspirations that rise and shine that deliberately opened my campaigner
strengths deepens my supraliminal inlightenmint that sweetens

My inner landscape to feel my frequencies of insight fires up my
incorruptible deathless wisdom as my precious mystical magic energizes
my trendsetter profundity feeling my omnipotent daredevilry clears

My state-of-the-art nomadic audacity to understand and value
listening witnessing and hearing my imaginative insight from the
unexampled unexplainable unknown clairvoyants floating through

The universe unlocks my nunow prowess as I now understand and
admire my fiery freedoms of everlasting pansophy that dares my eternal
animated trailblazer hutzpah lionizing enterprising savvy steam heating

My hellraisers energy aggrandizing troublemaker ingenuity niyama's gut
sense to raise and shine from within me maturing elicit understanding
and admiration for my deathless wisdom is my forever foresight now

Lighting up my paths nunow nirvana I travel now through eternity as
fly on my onward and upward gleaming my divine white light lionized
intrinsic enlightenment escalating my entertainer's sassy audacity

Lumens awe inspiring trail boss nerve gallantly clears away my
self-taught ignorance because keen-witted get n go initiates my
clairvoyant curiosity to run freely through my oracle omnificence

As I feel my perky pioneering wit awesomely ambles me up my
trails of triumph with a valorous vigor that lets my fly potentate
panache that dances me through life with the greatest of ease

As I expand of accomplished sovereign energy admitting to me myself
and I that I encompass the trendsetting tenacity to energize my wise that
unlocks typhoons of triumph excites my entrepreneurial fertility initiates

My campaigner's pizzazz and ultrautopian fortes to saunter through
life beaming my inlightened spiritual splendor expressing my
deathless wisdom through everlasting canonized classy inspirations

I soar of stupendous optimism appreciating everything with
heart gratitude as I say thank you to all expressing my classy
sovereign gallant gratitude to all people and the cosmos

As I bow expressing my bold optimistic moneymaker chi opening
me myself and I to my received lavish endless money flow and
tranquil life of leisure as I cleared my heart love to shine from me

As my liberated soul splendor warms earthly airwaves of praise
for everybody as I listen to invisible dreamers of the cosmos
expanding my deathless wisdom eloquently expressing

My endless inspirations daylighting jovial celebrations of hellacious
feeling unlimited nirvana flow through me to the universe
now and forever more I soar of spirit simplicity shining

My mystical poise lighting up idyllic colorful imaginative treasures
yazzajazzes my life of luxurious bliss boldly luminates my intrinsic
serendipitous smile that gleams my esteemed gratitude

Nunow Rave

I awakened to my nunow rave of numinous utopian nirvana optimizes
wisdom rebelliously aggrandizing visionary enterprising reveries
frees me to fathom and esteem my dreams are my nunow rave

As I admire and applaud my sovereign sass of my nunow rave of
visionary bravery to understand and concede all my life events
are/were momentary whether the events were uplifting

Downward spiraling or whatever unsheathed my confidence and
courage to realize and value all my previous life events are my present
moment memories that I embrace and face here and now entrusting

My nuwow rave unhampered me to understand and admire my
life events were/are good bad or indifferent as I now understand
and divulge I discharged and disconnected all my vengeful

Feelings revengeful emotions and raucous rhetoric here and now
releasing and dissolving my rear-view mirror sneers as I brashly
discharged and disconnected all of yesterday's vindictive vandals

Into extinction as I avow my adventurous vigor optimizes my wild
blue yonder curiosity unleashed my clever candor to understand
and esteem my memories from my previous life events are up and

Running interjecting what my subconscious programming feels
will keep me safe in my present moment as my subconscious
programming instinctively controls my life so everything

That occurred yesterday reoccurs in the present moment as I now
realize and admit my past events were like a ship passing in the night
as the unsavory memories are still active unknowingly control

My daily escapades that occur and happen in real time with
events that show up invited or uninvited that instantly create an
uncomfortable and unfamiliar that spark my emotions and

Feelings that trigger subconscious programming and memory mind
reactions or responses from previous situations as my subconscious
programming controls my thoughts so I fall back into prior events

That encompassed the same type of circumstances as I tumbled
back into the feelings emotions and thinking I taught myself to go
dark instantly as I now realize and admit whatever I talk about

Internally and externally good bad or uninteresting I manifest that
into my life escapades so now I realize and admit I taught myself to
latch onto all my unsavory events more avoiding the life escalating

Energy because the unsavory was my comfort zone I now admit and
divulge I fall prey to my self-induced pessimistic prattle rattling my
cage of rat a tat crap that made my life a never-ending struggle

In my subconscious programming and thinking mind because my
subconscious programming grasped struggle was my comfort zone
as I imbedded snapshots of struggle or whatever was unsettling

Until I dethroned yesterday's control so I addressed and discharged
everything involved in all unsavory situations then confessed
and disconnected all the pessimism and agony involved in

My past experiences then expressed and released all my torment
cynicism and narcissism with appreciation and love to the universe's
airwaves instantly opened my emancipating elegance to experience

My present moment gifts rainbowed my liberating charm colored the
heavenly skies with my nuwow rave of brave beams my numinous
nous that brightly blessed the world populace with nowborn

Ingenious wisdom inspiration and innovative wit clears the universe's
frequencies for people to hear and utilize supernatural sapience
painted ultramodern imagery and optimist oratory within me

Myself and I that unsheathed my trailblazer audacity to listen to
the inaudible that opened my eyes to see my invisible scenery of my
dreamers' paradises that elucidated my listeners lore dazzlingly

Cleared my fashion designers' eyes to see my splendid scenarios
of my nunow rave that scintillated celebratory entrepreneurial
nous ascends my revolutionary idealist's omnificence signifies

My wise whimsical journey clearing the way for me to understand and
admire my humor and fun promptly undid the pooh of the stew of
memory minds instantly intertwining my ultra-serendipitous felicity

With my supernatural grit get and go unleashing my glitzy ritzy
stylish savvy clears the way for me to understand and admire my
nunow rave releases me and frankly discharged my stress disengaged

My memories of being attached to my scaredy cat emotions and my
fraidy cat feelings instantly unlatched my omnipresent trailblazers'
intrepid oomph nobly styles my innate utopian spontaneity

Canonizes imaginative enthusiastic savvy that magnifies animated
enterprising brilliance that I rousted out my revolutionary resolve to
evolve of effrontery vigor optimizing lionhearted verve enthuses

My intrinsic synchronicity to fathom and admire the treasured
blessings of my life as I let fly my nunow rave unrestrained my
fame and fortune frontiersman fervency that dances my majestic

Gratitude decrees Infinite Spirit I give thanks for my regal rich moxie
personifies my knighted credence to opening the way for me to grasp
my everyday life encounters with a galvanizing gallantry to stand tall

Head high knees straight to witness all my experiences gleams my
guru designer daredevilry to look straight into the eyes of every test
sending forth a laser beam of bravery and spirited wisdom blasting

Every challenge to smithereens authorizing me to see taste smell hear
feel and expansively experience my imaginative opulence of every
second of my life as I drink fine wines of bountiful bliss feeling

My prime-time divine dreamers' breezes of abundance as I sit on the
Riviera watching the mystique of the Mediterranean on a clear warm
spring day with mother nature showing all her glamorous elegance

In a pristine perfect way as I bask in the sun of my divine right to
rest relax and be excessively rich that expresses my fanciful panorama
views that vividly articulates rabble-rousing dexterous wizardry

That expands the universe into my vibrant villa of never-ending
flow of plush prosperity in a regal extraordinary way as I sunbath
on the beaches in the south of France I witness wave after wave

Of money flow into my bank accounts in an illuminated loving
way feeling my sprees of spiritual peace that streams effervescent
eloquence swishes my kevalin (liberated soul) revelations

To masterfully understand I have forever experienced a continuous
now as I let fly my nunow rave brightly and boldly ignited my
light of curiosity straightforwardly expands me out of yesterday

Relishing and embellishing my here and now wows my thrillpower
loving my present moment unique mystical endeavors forever
awakens my adventurous soul salsas my spicy enticing

Enterprising energies to rise and shine electrifying my nowbirthed
luminary loyalty that dances my honour and integrity through
all phases of my amazing life experiences because

My emotions fervor feelings subconscious celebrations unconscious
lore and superconscious splendor powered up my brainpower
that brilliantly rainbows animated inspirational nibbana

Poetically ornate's my winners' eloquent revelations elucidates
my innate brainprowess charms my empire builders' brilliance
revolutionizes my adroit artistes nerve entices my pioneering omnific

Humor that inspires my explorer's mystical spontaneity saunters
me onto my heavenly paradises gleams my fun of my sun fluency
as I am sitting in my rocking chair of lush tranquility

Optimizing revolutionary nirvana as I awakened to my live
is momentary events to test me to be the best that brashly
energized my seer's tenacity now and forever more I soar

Of my energized farseeing feelings and futuristic emotions to
energizing my subconscious celebrations that energized my
brain frequencies of innovative foresight ignited light of love

I Personalwise to Depersonalize

I intentionally gave me myself and I permission to love be loved
healthy wealthy wise and enjoying my lavish endless cashflow to relax
rest and be extremely rich savoring my cosmic serenity illumes

My clear blue heavenly skies for me to fashionably design color
and paint my pristine dreams life of lavish luxury and amazing
accomplished outcomes as I deliberately and instantly received

My lavish endless cashflow now and forever more I flow and glow
of gusto gratitude and awesome ascending appreciation as my
sassy classy sovereignty electrifies my nunow splendor for me

To let fly my omniscient omnificence to outline draw and sketch
my dreamers' paradises on my earthly horizons and third eye movie
screen as I embellished a helluva of good time as I unleashed

My personalwised spunk to instantly and caringly discharge my
stressed-out emotions to zero to have zippo effect on my life now
as I energized my personalwise bravery to nobly disconnect

All my agonizing feelings from my life purging all my feelings
to zero to having zip effect on my life today expands energizes
and enterprises everything I know into pacesetter wisdom

As I masterfully admire my everlasting insight instantly waltzes my
imaginative spectaculars dawns omnificent magnificence unsheathes
my innerprising wisdom that is my unattached utopian lore enthuses

My debonair questionnaire flair dared me to expand energize and
enterprise my nirvana emotions and inlightened feelings to grab
the mane and swing aboard my runaway mustang bravura

As I ride hell bent for election to effortlessly lope onto my serene pristine Garden of Eden sensing peaceful festivities embellishing my elegantly divine enlightenmint neon's my sweetened personalwise

Spontaneity to understand and admire I intrinsically authorized my past to be characterless featureless blameless shameless faceless nameless and depersonalized to instantly dethrone discharge

Disconnect release and dissolve all my pain and agony everything and everybody I blamed for my past and current life situation because I was trying to cover up and hide silly selfish shame went extinct now

As I boldly bravely and responsibly depersonalized my past in a blast of bravado brilliance as I say so long to all my pain agony fears and scaredy cat bratiness in loving way with class and integrity

I enthusiastically personalwised my life extravaganzas as I personalwise my life I instantly stopped thinking about the people involved in my life to intuitively investigate my life events

As I now realize and concede people come and go as that event was streaming my life energizing gumption as I now shout the universes airwaves I am responsible and accountable for

My interactions and the way I respond to the events and the people as I admit and grasp I taught myself to interrogate the other person then investigate the situation to uncover and discover all

The ways the situation expanded and glorified my wisdom energized my inspiration and enterpized my innovative gifts to galvanize inborn foresight tantalizing supernatural listening

Optimizing imaginative wizardry because I now realize and admire I escalate my innate talent as I listen then I hear my seers savvy energize my gut gumption enterprising trailblazer

Talents electrifying my deliberate dexterous daredevilry to make
the people of my live events featureless faceless nameless shameless
blameless and depersonalized my past present and future enthuses

My gut acuity and instigator spunk to investigate my inner scenery
unlocking my imaginative extravaganzas to enthusiastically enjoy
my land of milk and honey as I pat myself on the back for trusting

My abilities as I fluently and intentionally expanded out of my
agonizing events to expand of optimistic grit that lets fly intrinsic
felicity to feel my inborn cheery investigator to bluntly query me

As I ask… How has hearing and feeling all my past self-inflicted
pain agony blame shame egoistical knowing revengeful thinking
vengeful thoughts trying to get even with somebody gossiper gunk
and my life was somebody else's fault that internally controlled me?

As I gutted up to grasp and concede I embedded my thinking
knowing and memories from my ambushing pessimism and trolling
cynicism from my childhood encounters thru todays scenarios

That jumped up created my hurtful feelings and painful emotions
from my myopic insecurity and my corrupting immaturity
that wrung me out in doubt pouting about whatever

I thought somebody did me was a lewd fib I lived and told myself
died yesterday so I daylight I boldly and brightly stood up looked
into my lionhearted liberating mirror today standing tall shoulders

Back knees straight looked straight into my soul's eyes to surprise
my soul said stop the rat a tat crap thinking somebody did
something to me freed my gut gumption to give me a swift kick

In the butt to strut my bright ubiquitous trendsetting torchbearer
sassy tenacity revolutioneyeszing ultramodern thaumaturgy
wizardry to understand thaumaturgy is my miracle magician says

Abracadabra and my life of lavish leisure instantly appears and
that is my nunow wow way of life as my dharma dexterity lets fly
my charismatic charm magnetized the earth's airwaves and

My universe frequencies of financial freedom canonizing my
hellacious animated rapturous marriage harmonizing my heart
love intrinsic liberation health wealth stunning success and

My straight forward fortitude to say good bye yesterday and hello
to my head honcho emancipated lionhearted liberator that blatantly
my stouthearted warrior sat me down looked straight into

My eyes and began querying me then asked me How do/did I
blame people that were involved in my life situations for everything
allowed to occur? As my fanatic panic paranoia that exposed

My crabby worrywart hypocrisy as I fell prey to my inner disarray
speaking my pessimistic palaver internally created my cynical
mindset that infuriated my namby-pamby prattle for to ask me.

This question. How did trying to make other people responsible and
accountable for my current life situations smothered me heartache
and self-ingrained pain? That rattled my thinking and thoughts

Around like a BB in a box car darting from turmoil to torment to
fear and then back again frustrated and stressed me in pandering to
my subconscious programming is actually performing the task

I asked it to do is because I saying all these unsavory things about
myself and my subconscious thoughts that is want my subconscious
thought I wanted so now I unleashed my personalwise

To deliberating ask for exactly everything I desire and intentionally
speaking about me myself and I inspired awesome light of love as
I now realize and admit my personalwise wininity opens me

Myself and I to my pristine paradises of selflove selfrespect selfworth
and selfsovereignty standing tall looking life in the eye with my spry
straight-arrow fortitude streaming my stupendous trendsetter

Rabble rousing enterprising acumen masterfully invigorating
numinous grit get and go as I understand and relish my moviemaker
spirit puts challenges in front of me to discharge my pessimism to

The zero state audaciously turned on my hellraiser hutzpah that
hellaciously charges my troublemaker vigor to vibrantly instigate
my grinning optimistic resplendence pranced and enhanced

My straightforward spunk that unfunked my life because I now
participate and facilitate my optimistic wisdom and confidence to
be accountable and responsible for my life now and forever more

I soar classy stylish integrity showing the world my heart
of love because life is fun for me as I sail away of my yacht
of tranquility as the ocean waves are fans of serenity

Imagination

I now marvel to understand and esteem my numinous imagination escalates my day to day life with intuitive imagery that energized and enterprized my wisdom and inspiration expanding me thru life

Hearing and trusting my innovative fortitude that mystically and magically magnetizes my life with my visionary miracles that arrive on my third eye movie screen from out of everywhere dares me

To rise up and out of thinking memory mind that untwines my rhyming prime time optimist's wizardry geysers my spontaneous quixotic innovations neon's my splendorous acumen that opens

My gut gumption to understand and esteem my shrewd imagination lets me float above my current life situations like floating over the Grand Canyon free of everything as I now fathom and esteem

The Colorado River mirrors my day to day life as I opened my marvelous ingenuity to feel and witness me floating in midair in the center of the Grand Canyon over the Colorado River admiring

The colorful scenery and the endless panorama views as my intuitive imagination I simply relaxed and rested in midair as I am effortlessly floating over the picturesque Colorado River as my life is a colorfully

Ceremoniously mystique and magically unique mirroring the Grand Canyon and Colorado River authentically mirror's my life's twists and turns with thunderstorms that awakened my artistic verve and

Colorful scenery of my dreams as I float effortlessly along my animated trailblazer brilliance awakens me to grasp and value my imagination is my nomadic nurturing nirvana to naturally

Optimize ubiquitous savvy realizing and esteeming my mystical
imagination energizes my ultramodern peerless urbane fame freed
my animated moviemaker pizzazz as I fathom and esteem

My imagination is my unattached visionary vigor and clairvoyant
inlightenmint sweetens my artistic scenarios lets fly the images of
my adventurous glamorous intuitive nous {mother-wit} animates

My topflight innovative omnificence nourishes my life of unrestrained
vacationers' vitality because I now realize to expand through life
I adhere to my soothsayer imagination pacesetter poise and

Clear-sighted inspirations galvanized my invincible intuition enlivens
my initiator innovations thrusting and trusting my torchbearer
faculties to witness and experience my nunow acuity gleams

My sassy classy vanguard flair endeared me to my clairvoyant curiosity
deliberately unlocked and let fly my rendezvousing revolutionary
insight optimizes sovereign inborn temerity yazzapizzazzes

My snazzy thrillpower to rise above and float over my thinking
knowing memory mind unbinding my memory minds feeling lively
omnific perspicacity tantalize my get n go that instantly unwinds and

Intertwines my prime-time ingenuity illuminated my divine flight
of felicity lauds innate glamorous heavenly treasures flow and glow
gusto's my mammoth money flow that instantly surprised

Me with my fabulous life of leisure that unleashed my nowborn
innovations that turned on my brainpower invigorated my artistic brain
agility to brilliantly revolutionize my dynamic designers' daredevil

Spectaculars for me to relish and embellish my plush lush tropical
paradises in a gigantic valiant optimistic way as I feel hear witness
taste touch and smell my beautiful rose fields of extravagant

Riches because I trusted my imaginative wizardry unleashed my instinctive ground-breaking clairvoyance as I marvel at my life of serene lush leisure as my pioneering ingenuity showed me the way

To my serene blossoming Garden of Eden experiencing dazzling exquisite heaven on earth heydays sassily surfing on my seas of stunning success feeling quietly wealthy and peacefully healthy

As I asked me How was I afraid to utilize my imagination to expand out of challenges and chaos I faced throughout my day? As I awakened to masterfully admire my imagination wisdom inspiration

Intuition innovation trailblazer talents are my native kevalin keys of free that spontaneously declared me to ask How will utilizing my imagination expand me through life in an easier sunnier way?

As I dance energetically celebrating revolutionary endeavoring eloquence expressing my luminary lyrics of liberation to instantly harken my everlasting verses of wisdom from universes frequencies

Of freedom feeling rebellious electrifying enlightenmint daylighted my omnipresent magnetism invigorated my imaginative spiritual charm as my fashion designer deliberately elucidates inspiring insightful

Nowborn empire building acumen influenced my designed Shangri-La upshots on my third eye movie screen effortlessly strolls me through life trusting my impeccable up-to-the-minute visionary verve

Illuminates my spirit savoir-faire flair saunters me up trails of triumph because I trusted my trail boss leadership rancher wit pathfinder foresight and globetrotter gumption that unlocked and unblocked

My effervescent utopian courage lionizing clever kinetic clairvoyance stimulates my trailblazer talents dawning unfathomable nunow wow brilliance optimizing ceremonious kevalin charm lightens

Brightens and electrifies my magical mystique instantly flashes my unique ultrabright nibbana (is the highest spiritual state) innovates quick-witted ubiquitous utopian lore opening my divine design

That spiritually intertwines all phases of my amazing life that tenaciously turned on my rambling rabble-rousing gumption as I stroll through day to day celebrations I uncover and discover

My trailbreaker forte's that salsas me through my challenges chaos tragedies and day to day life with ease as I sense my sovereign grandeur as I now masterfully value my artistic powers

That asked me... How did my parents and societies way of life disconnect me imagination and innovative savvy? Invigorated my adventurous gumption my splendid accomplishments

Bountifully blessing my nunow felicity avows my imagination opened my heart eyes souls' ears spiritual touch exquisite taste splendorous smell of walking through fields of blossoming four-leaf

Clover enjoying luxurious tranquility sensing I am well-heeled and heart healthy as I bravely released and dissolving all my thinking knowing and memories from the past because I now admit and

Value I will never move out of yesterday or away from my ancestor anchors by grasping this I instantly unbridled and energized my heart brain communication sensing my effrontery emotions trusting

Listening and witnessing my nowfound fortitude entrusting and thrusting my imagination into my life expanding ventures that instigates my animated imagery that colors my life with

My dreamer's greenery feeling and living my loving vigorous prosperous way of life that flows through me my dreamers' paradises with my head high shoulder back walking tall because

My imagination is my individual moxie applauding my audacious
vim and vigor invigorating nomadic adventurous tenacity
instigating optimists' nerve to never swerve or sway away from

My challenge's chaos or unsavory untimed situations because I now
realize and admit I can never be negative about anything when my
imagination wisdom inspiration intuition inventive wit and trailblazer

Talents are engaged and escalating my innate pacesetter lore lionizing
optimistic outcomes with dynamic insight as I now masterfully
love my imagination dissolves political correctness energizes

My unconquerable imagination as I AM listening endorsing and
intentionally hearing and trusting my ingenuity inspiration intuition
innovative wit that engage and energize my intrinsic sage electrifies

My revolutionary lore lionizes optimistic omniscient kinetic insight
unbridled my inborn verve that forever unsheathes my valiant
grit opened my heart to show me love so I show the world love

I AM Grounded

I AM grounded and grinning exposing my visionary magician with a magic wand of wonderful instantly illuminates my mystical stroll through life gleaming my serendipitous splendor frontrunner

Foresight spine tingling bravura electrified my clairvoyant curiosity gifted me with my peerless prowess to wow my trailblazer legacies because my feet are firmly planted in and on mother earth

As mother earth is my incorruptible and unbreakable foundation I feel under me and as my truss of pure love I walk on now and forever more as I AM Grounded trusting mother earth as I AM intentionally

Listening honouring and trusting my heavenly father's prescience (presh-ee-*uh*ns) embellishing my spiritual maturity to expand energize enterprise my experiences of nomadic ventures and stunning

Glory because I AM grounded of health wealth unconditional love designer's lore unrestrained extravagance and mammoth endless cascading cash flow with everlasting classy humble Thank You

As I AM a Grounded Spirit beaming my heart love through me to the world lionizing optimistic vibrant stamina that emancipated my grounded gumption that instantly and bluntly unleashed

My Iwon ardor as I let fly my animated artistic clairvoyance that cleared my savvy seers' eyes to witness and admire my nunow wow that wonderfully opened my whimsical spontaneity to go

With flow boating on my rivers of robust riches that I effortless float on feeling laudable opulent affluence titillating my ultra-bright felicity electrified my savior faire emotions and fancy-free feelings

That are bonded with mother earth harkens my smiling heavenly
father dancing with my spiritual maturity of majestic ascendancies
tantalizing ultra-resplendent intuitive trailblazer yazzapanache

To swiftly stop accepting my everyday life through my self-taught stuff
to admit and understand being grounded to mother earth stopped
me from being perched on earth and wandering through life

Aimlessly and feeling lost tossed and bossed by my life events because
I lacked feeling connected to my earth source so now I AM grounded
so I discharged and dissolved yesteryears crying in beer sneers

My nunow optimism magnetizes my nowborn opportunities letting
fly my nunow wow my wherewithal optimizes wanders curiosity to
flow through me unleashing my nomadic nerve to witness my life

Of vivacious leisure on my plush paradises because I AM thee
listening enthusiast expanding natural tenacity hellaciously
unleashing my regal rich moxie magnetizes my cosmic celebrations

As float through Milky Way with a rush of feel sassy classy energy
just as my audacious adventurous wit electrifies enterprising get-up-
and-go arouses the utopian wit as feel my grounded power propel me

To unleash my innovative genius in an authentic affluent way
authorizing me to swim in a pool of milk and honey delights
enjoying life in a fun of the sun Shangri a La way awakened

My copious magnificence titillates farseeing luminary eloquence
harkens my smiling heavenly father fervency to dance with tantalizing
my ultra-instinctive sassy innovative acumen skillfully tantalizing

My globetrotter yazzapanache that deliberately detached me from my
daily encounters opens the way for me to facilitate and participate
my nowfound foresight that I heard and witnessed throughout

My daily voyages of awakening my daring aware troublemaker
optimism that ignited my light of life untethered my heart
sovereignty and let fly my heart love magnifying my moneymaker

Magic because I witness I AM grounded vibrant valor galvanizes
revolutionary omnific ubiquitous nirvana daredevilry decrees
my sprees of feisty stylish pathfinder dexterity dawns

My risk takers credence empowers my inventors' abilities and
agility to feel my heart love that intentionally powered up my soul's
serenity to be at peace with myself to be at peace with my life and

To be at peace with other people to never ever get caught up in
their traumatizing stuff or any phase of their life or fall back into
my insecurities and immaturities of past instantly unlatched

My classy sassy savvy panache to understand and admire I AM
Grounded and esteeming my gleaming rebellious optimist's utopian
nerve spawns my glistening rapturous state-of-the-art savvy

As I feel my shrewd sovereignty flows through my veins of valorous
emancipated inspired nowborn serendipitous bliss that streams
thru all phases of my amazing life as I now masterfully admire

I AM amazing trusting my awesome grit get and go feeling my
Grounded Grinning Gumption titillates and excites my championing
charm catapulted my canny hellacious sovereign mystique

Of my unique piquancy as I feel grounded expressing my awe-
inspiring nunow bravura as I audaciously allow my feelings and
emotions to be faceless blameless and shameless energizing

My dreamers' picturesque power and panorama scenery of my
designed life as the images of my past are featureless nameless and
characterless and blameless exhilarates my pristine inner landscape

With numinous love painting my desired life as I now masterfully
admire my feelings and emotions to embrace my grounded
grinning gumption as my vibrant cavalry riding with

My illuminated imagination wisdom inspiration intuition
innovation trailblazer talent that powered up my brainpower turned
on my brainprowess as I now realize and admire I grounded

In my artistic acuity to understand and esteem the universe is my
canvas for me to paint my dreams unleashes my Rembrandt prowess
painting the heavens with my brilliant copious cornucopia coloring

The skies with my vibrant life of luxurious leisure unshackling my
invincible optimism grounded the world to flow of opulent opulence
in an artistic astute way as I sail the Queen Mary of lavish avalanches

Of affluent abundances in a picture-perfect way I am grounded so
my imagination initiates galvanizing unexampled mystical prosperity
tantalizing artistic omnificence neon's my drawers' dexterity and

Designer's vigor expresses my ingenious gifts that unbridles my
inventor's foresight tantalizing stunning success feeling I AM
blessed with ingenious emotions as I masterfully admire

I candidly communicate with mother earth heavenly father
and spiritual supremacy traveling through life with an
electromagnetic force that magnetizes universes airwaves with

My intuitive innovative epiphanies gleaming esteemed trendsetter
dreamers daredevilry dawning audacious resplendent eloquence
declaring effervescent visionary inventors' luminous reveries

Yazzadazzles my canny classy selfworth that beams my glitzy ritzy
resolve to evolve of grounded grinning glamor steam heats my hearts
elegant animated trendsetter serendipitous wealth and health

As I Am Grounded I AM grinning listening smiling in absorbing fresh artistic lore because my life is a mystery filled with riddles for me to expand through broadening

My emblazing leadership fortitude lights up the heavens with my sovereign sapience opening the listening prowess within me to understand I AM Grounded as I listen to expand my wisdom

As I enjoy feeling I AM grounded embellishing hellacious health wealth and success in blessed way as I express my wisdom with debonair flair dancing with heart nirvana in a sunny splendid way

My energized acumen and elegant enterprising prowess experiencing my life of Riley in a great big bold bright way now and forever more I AM Grounded of my romanticist bravery

Living on my dreamers' pristine paradises feeling my heavenly suns relaxing rays of serene pure peace flow through me as I am grinning of gratitude smiling of appreciation feeling loved

NO

I now understand relish and embellish the wisdom inspiration high-spirited tenacity and confidence of saying NO is understanding and admiring the powerful purpose of NO is NO and never reply...

To any a why questions or any question after saying NO as I awakened to understand and esteem I can never say NO to the outside world until I can say NO to my bad habit's poor behaviors worn

Out patterns and everything desire to have disconnected and discharged from my life as I woke to this nowborn bravura awakened my intrinsic sunrise wise embraced my brilliant bravado

As I was out and about my mind wanted to do something then my nowbirthed spunk stoutheartedly said NO then my inner saboteur said Why? Then my numen nerve forthrightly and fiercely said stop

To my inner treasonous that always tries to talk me out of the higher road and into doing what I was craving to do then I would do it then I would walk away with my head down frowning and hiding

In my worrywart wimpy despair because my insecurity and immaturity disliked me hearing or saying NO until yesterday as I disconnected and discharged the inner selfishness about hearing or saying NO

As I now realize and admit when I respect and honour NO within me myself and I then I respect and honour hearing NO from other people in a thankful way as I now realize and admit I disliked hearing NO

So disliking hearing NO created wound emotions and feeling as I now admit I was fearful of NO as I ask How is hearing or saying NO the highest outcome for all people involved in certain situations?

So I awakened to being aware of the liberating lore of NO because NO is saying YES to something greater in my life and a yazzasnazzy yes to me myself and I so I stopped being afraid of hearing or saying NO

Went away yesterday as now grasp the authority of NO instantly opened my hellraiser hutzpah to understand before I can say NO in my physical world I have to encompass gut gall to say NO to myself and

I and to stand pat on NO through situation to the end because I rouse this morning with an honourable inner hellion rebellion energizing my nowfound fortitude to understand and esteem whenever I say NO

It's a gracious pointed bold NO telling the other party to just go away and play anywhere but where I am as I stand in my leader's poise wisdom and confidence of my NO its NO because Yes and NO are

The standalone words as I say NO with charisma and charm instantly disarmed my unwanted habits undesirable behaviors and my unsavory past that released my intestinal fortitude to never have

To set a boundary in my external landscape because my spine-tingling NO unlocks and let's fly my courage confidence and unconquerable energy to say NO Thank You to the person or event

That is/was never for my highest outcome because I say NO and NO alone is my bona fide boundary inside me and my physical world to realize and admire I say NO to everything

I never wanted is instantly saying YES to my awesome fun of the sun splendor I embedded because as said good bye to the delusional despair unpleasant memories now as I enjoy telling the world about

My prime-time fun experiences yet I admit and grasp I tried to hide all my pain anger and frustrations falsely putting on my bragger's bullying act walking around like a dipshit acting like zippo bothered me was

Me deceiving me because the charged emotions and connected feelings are traumatizingly anchored to the life experiences and still controlled the daily encounters as I tried the bozo braggers act and

It was the most delusional victimizing cracker jack crap I ever have done or did were attached distressed emotions tied me to my larcenist deceits that zippo bothered me stopped yesterday as I sense

My visionary vitality embraces my flawless feelings and faultless emotions as my spirit connected me to my utopian universe brightly unleashes my nowborn imaginative visions optimizing

My innate life's rainbow bold spectaculars I embrace on my daily voyages because I encompass the stamina to expand out of my fear and falling prey to the attached rat a tat crap that kept me stuck

In the melodrama of mediocrity with the shaming feelings blaming emotions and habitual programming kept spinning me in deception and wallowing around and lapsing into my worn-out overthinking

That kept me trying to change my thinking yet my thinking knowing memory mind stayed as I trust and utilize my sword of straightforward sapience cutting off any and all questions from everybody and

Anybody that is to insecure and immature to hear and grasp NO is NO so when somebody asks why or any other question about the NO the forthright response is NO as I realize and value Yes and NO are

The only standalone words I ever express are Yes and NO as both words require zero explanation validation reason or anything so now I understand and admire to say NO to everything I never wanted

In my life or in my physical world as I flat out say NO to my unwanted rat a tat crap that I used to talk myself out of my desired life by caving into the inner larcenist palaver and procrastinating heckler

As I would cave into the delusional hypocrisy and illusional arrogance
of myself all passed away today as I instantly say Yes to my dreams
affluent gifted outcomes and tranquil luxurious leisure feeling

Alive and thriving unleashed my energized felicity electrified my
elegant emotions of my nowborn inlightenmint embellishing my
nunow wow of wonderful omniscient world of wealth embracing

My radical regal lore dancing on my moon of magnificent optimistic
omnipotence thrills my numinous nerve to brashly express a sharp yes
to my beautiful nowborn lush abundances marvelously witnessing

My bountiful blessings from the universe now and forever more
I soar of selfworth because I stopped giving a rat's ass whether
people get mad because I said NO the answer is a definitive NO

With humble gallantry because my enterprising NO's optimistically
energized my Nowfangled Opportunities as I now master and honour
my core values as I awaken to my effrontery epicenter trusting

My straightforward backbone brilliance to understand and admire my
spirit savvy strolls me through life as I now understand I never ever
have to set external boundaries when my heart hutzpah's breathes

My light of liberation my inner candid enthusiasm lights up intestinal
fortitude excited my stouthearted self-esteem that immediately
beamed my bright enlightened aura spiritedly stimulated my innate

Potentate prowess to admit and master my preeminent poise
comprises my wise surprising sagacity to say NO in my internal
landscape as my heart and brainpower coherence show the external

World NO with unselfish love I instilled within me myself and I
promptly unleashes my rebellious resolve to trust my trailboss spirit
to never be a bragger to showing my humble honcho brio exhibiting

My leadership wisdom with listeners spontaneity to harken my
hellraisers will to say NO with nerve and YES with stouthearted spunk
and classy sass as my enthusiastic insight let's fly my numen nerve

Opens my heart to my lavish endless life of tranquil luxurious lifestyle
as my audacious acumen stoutheartedly expressed to me NO is my
stand-alone boundary because the instant as I now mastered and

Esteem I say NO and never reply to why or any question on the reason
I said NO I now reply with straightforward courageous NO now and
forever more I soar of NO as my Nowborn Optimistic Nerve Opens

My rebellious wisdom to flow showing my sassy classy selfworth to
the world with beaming dignity I salsa of sovereign adventurous lore
stimulating amazing sightseeing ventures loving life as life loves me...

As I now masterfully say Yes to my life of leisure as I blatantly
say NO to my selfish habits pity me patterns and boneheaded
behaviors to instantly savor my serendipitous splendor

Rebellious Vocabulary

I feel my spicy spirited magical mystique rockets my Rebellious
Vocabulary that lightning bolts my mystical moxie lionizing my
thaumaturgy mojo instantly let's fly my unique visionary gifts

Of gallant internal fervor tenacity sassily titivating my vanguard
fascination unrestrained my guru talents tantalizing my inspirational
expressions that electrifying Xanadu poetic revelations energizes

My snazzy spine-tingling phrases optimizes my nunow vigor that
energized my risk taker adrenaline that turned on my oracle oratory
optimism energized my pert linguistic wizardry unlocked

My undomesticated omnificence that triggered my leadership
tenacity to understand and admire my rebellious vocabulary
instantly excited my rabble-rousing resolve that liberated me from

The society influenced speaking and self-taught nagging and
bragging words that I selfishly spoke inside me that were horribly
hokey poking me with a pity me palaver that effortless departed

My life yesterday and forever as I immediately awoke to hear
me express I AM hellaciously dynamic dawning yazzapoetic
nibbana animating mystical inspiration celebrating

My selfworth with fireball felicity whimsically whirled my revolutionary
dreamers' splendor excited my adventurous ardor opened the door
for me to soar feeling alive with thriving entertainers' eloquence...

As I now grasp and esteem my inspired lyrics of luminary
yazzapanache rev up my intuitive canonizing spectaculars to
flow on third eye movies screen on the heavenly skies and

On my earthly horizons of my life excites my snazzy jazzy jubilees
of jovial utopia boldly inventing life's enterprising endeavors
with an optimist's essence gallantly invigorating sassy

Tenacity to rise energizing my divine daredevilry sprees my lyricist
acuity buzzes my vim and vigor to look my extravaganzas in the
eye with gunslinger spunk with warrior aura streaming from

Me unsheathes my maverick energy to understand and admire my
life experiences that enthused my maestro muse that polished my
wanders wisdom to expand me and dreams thru to my amazing

Gifted results utilizing my rebellious vocabulary revering emancipated
brilliance energizing love lionizing imaginative utopian savvy
visualizing opulent clairvoyance animating bold ultramodern

Adventures yazzajazzes my canny innovator that let fly my clever
endeavoring bliss that awakened my gladiator gumption that
electrifies my moviemaker moxie to understand and admire

I AM the producer director and famous mega movie star of my
life brilliant extravaganzas as I now realize and esteem words
excite my nowfangled energy optimizing my ornery optimism

To write and speak to the now that electrifies my futuristic fortunes
because I stopped writing and speaking to what I know opened my
auditory ardor to soar of spirited oratory acumen revolutionizing

My dreamers enterprising wizardry because I now express my
rebellious vocabulary pizzazz's instantly turned on my brilliant light
of excitement feeling the sweet nectars of nirvana flow through

My rabble-rousing cells of hellraiser hutzpah candidly celebrating
my life events as my celebrating emotions and festive feelings
extravaganzas electrifies my spring flings titillating

My stupendous sightseer splendor to understand and admire my
expansionism of my intrinsic spiritual maturity magnetizes the earths
airwaves with my dreams electromagnetic forces instantly manifests

My Garden of Eden delights as my outlaw optimism unleashes my
troublemaker expressions animated my amazing crazy candor that
tells me to write and speak to my dreams dawning revolutionary

Festivals actuating maverick sass to stop kissing my pasts ass
ignited my thrilling visionary vitality awakened my hellraiser
heart and sassy soul's spunk airmails my spirit charm through

The universes airwaves courageously harmonizeyezes amazing
resplendent magnificence to fill the earth's atmosphere endearing
me to feel rebelliously blessed with vibrant resiliency

To see my life through enlightened eyes to see through the mysteries
of my life's messes that magically escalates spirit literacy lighting
up my internal treasured imaginative articulation revving

Up ascending clever yazzawizardry unleashing my zealous zest
to understand and esteem I express inspired fiery foresight that
ignites my bright inlightened hoot n hollering chutzpa

That unhooked the books of the school system as an absolute so
I unpunctuated my writings unprogramming societies systems of
follow the herdocracy of turdocracy kicking all the not words out

Of my life let fly my rebellious vocabulary as I stopped trying to
change my life in any way opening my gut gumption to expand of
my dreams energizing my charming wise perspicacity exciting

My enterprising wizardry feeling and hearing my liberating lore to
sense the fascination of my unique mystique's trusting my mystical
magical maestro communicates my miraculous magnificent

Eloquence expresses my rebellious vocabulary unleashing my
visionary omnific clever acumen brightly unsheathed my literary
autonomous yazzapizzazz that spiritually awakened me

To understand and embellish speak of my dreams the life
I desire to experience and my moneyed up accomplished
accomplishment with inspiration wisdom and celebration feeling

My robust outcomes with emotions of accomplishment grasping and
admiring my hellraiser hutzpah speaking my rebellious vocabulary
as I bask of my rainbow brilliance to understand and admire

My nunow wow shows me my life of my lavish endless luxurious
bliss that kisses my me with unselfish and unconditional love
now and forever more I speak unique hellraiser crazy

Celebrations enjoying my life free of caring what other people
think because my thinking created my insecurity and immaturity
as my inspiration wisdom and celebrations rocketed

My royal acumen and noble nerve that daringly salsas me
myself and I to my Shangri La paradises as I roll the dice that
intentionally enticed my immaculate charm that energized

My ultrautopian fervor acumen whooshes of my spicy dreamer's
optimistic mystical abundances dared me to ascend of my miraculous
enterprising reveries stimulating my inborn innovator nerve boldly

My wanders wise geysers my esteemed gleaming dreams
romancing my electrifying autonomous mystique magnificently
yazzadazzles my enterprising pizzazz jazzes my sassy savvy

As I love life and life loves me myself and I as I beam my sassy
sexy sovereignty to the universe for all to feel free enjoying love
health wealth and success in a bold bright energetic way

Gunslinger Brilliance

I now fathom and admire my gunslinger brilliance to understand
and esteem it was never the fastest gunslinger that won the
battle it was always the most willing to stand in the face

Of adversity and controversy with an conquerors versatility that
walked away from challenges so Infinite Spirit I AM feeling my
gunslinger brilliance that opened my will to understand and esteem

I have never ever been angry at anything in the outside world
even though I thought I was and I acted like I was all the went
away yesterday as I awakened to my gunslinger brilliance that

I was angry at me myself and I as I now admit I was angry at
something inside me that I was unwilling to expand out of it was
my soft addiction to my comfort zone so I now realize and admit

To expand of my optimistic felicity to understand and concede my
outside world shows me my good bad and ugly stuff inside me the
bad and the ugly are for me to masterfully mature my majestic

Magnificent leadership and the glorious gusto of my heart and
soul as I ceremoniously celebrate my healthy wealthy loving life in
a big bold bright bold way as I now aggrandize and appreciate

My newfound fortitude to admit and get I stopped caving into my
outside world controlling me to instantly escalate my sovereign
prowess canonize my gunfighter wit to experience life inside out

With valorous dignity optimizing utopia treasures to revere eternal
appreciation streaming unexampled reveries titivate my intrinsic
wizardry that unleashed my gunslinger brilliance that embraced

My gunfighter mettle that stared and scared down all the sneering
backbiting bullshitters of the outside world spewing their ridiculing
drool of dipshit drudgery judging and poking fun at me for

Living beyond there know it all ignorant belligerence that keeps
them living inside there musty dusty egotistical cynicism scared of
everything that was unfamiliar because I now realize and value

Anything I ridicule or poke fun at is my insecurities and immaturities
shutting down me down internally masking the conceited despair
somewhere thinking life was never fair was my self-stained fallacies

I lived until yesterday as I blasted all the thieving fears scaredy
cat bratiness and arrogant ignorance to smithereens to instantly
trust my gunslinger brilliance brashly realizing and admire

My fiery gladiator oomph that neon's my charming spicy luminous
integrity nurturing glorious enterprising resplendence gleaming
my bodhi resolve invigorating luminary light instigated

My voyager's nous candidly excited my grit get and go that
energized my numen nerve enterprising my victor's wizardry frees
me to feel my stouthearted emotions of my gunslinger valor

To galvanize unfathomable numinous savvy lionizing internal daring
gumption extolling revolutionary liberation within me because
I now admit and get all my anger hate and stress are within

Me were created by me and were self-taught by me as I concede and
realize I used all dark despair as subconscious survival mechanisms I
taught myself to instigate selfish malice vandalism that overtakes

Me internally because I allowed the knowing thinking mind
and memorized thoughts from the external world control me yet
the external landscape has never stopped me from anything

I stopped myself internally by falling prey to believing what other people said then playing victim to my insecurities and immaturities trying to live in societies needy ways as I now grasp and concede

I tried to please others and tried to fit in with the most popular people was my lethargic self-impaired thinking of I was never good enough then memorizing habitual cynicism was the ruinous fabrications

That lewdly glued me to my never do delusions that I could never experience my dreams then I used ire dislike and backbiting bratiness to stay annoyed and lived inside the inane mundane prattle

That created the retaliatory retorts that I spewed to the physical world that kept me thinking I was tuff yet I felt the sham of shame biting me in the butt because I now grasp and concede

Whenever I'm angry at something in the physical world I now admit I'm disgusted and distrusting my inabilities that subconsciously controlled me myself and I stuck crying in

My sneering insecurities and incapacitating immature mockery about everything as I was conceitedly shocked when things went awry I would cry in beer blather getting all lathered up over zilch because

I was afraid of the situation and scared thinking I had to know more than the other person and be right so I got angry to cover up the lack of insight I sensed because I taught myself at a young age that

I knew everything and I was right about everything was the musty mockery that was embedded about my life situations I encountered that locked me into yesterday until my nunow wow dawned

My sunrise wizardry that awakened my cowboy up spunk to unfunk my life with sassy spunk and spicy savvy to stroll of spirit tenacity revering omnipotent luring love that energizes

The cosmic frequencies of lavish financial and personal freedoms
now and forever as I now understand and respect anger hate
jealousy competition and comparing myself to others was

My survival mode ridicule within me myself and I as I now
fly above the fray of my innermost fearful ridicule that I
spewed inside me gluing my in yesteryears sneers

All passed away now as I fiercely freed me to detach from outer
world rhetoric clearing my seers endearing energy to witness my day
to day life through luminous inspiration feeling ecstatic because

As I expand out of the know it all belligerence egotistical cynicism
and subconscious pessimism dissolving and dethroning the delusional
polarizing demising ways to expand of optimist's foresight

That ignites my rainbow light of holidaymaker lore that illuminates my
inspirations wisdom and celebrations that sensual wises my intuitive
landscape with panorama scenery of pristine peace and plush

Lush prosperity that opened my gut gumption to trust my
communicative skills listeners dexterity and trailblazer temerity that
unsheathed my triumphant confidence and pioneering courage

To trust my bright light of love angelically gleams my immaculate
imagination wisdom inspiration intuition innovative trendsetter talents
that immediately rockets my nunow wow through every phase

My gunslinger brilliance and gunfighter guts to stand in the
face of my life expanding situations with smile of stouthearted
mystical inspiration lionizing enterprising surprises to rise from

My divine outline I imprint with gusto in subconscious celebrations
galvanizing unexampled stupendous treasured opulence that
begins my swagger onto my winners walk of wealth health and

Innovative skills cleared the way for my nowbirthed iwiiitt to rise
and shine embellishing my copious accomplished upshots as I AM
daringly aware of my nowfangled (freshly fashioned scenarios) nirvana

As I calmly sitting in my rocking chair of ravishing bountiful ecstasy
as I feel relaxed rested and rich as I grasp this idea I unleashed
my stylish abilities trusting my futuristic guru to draw design

Color and paint my supernatural universe with out of this world
charismatic charm as I now trust my inner self worth to expand
energize and enterprise my lavish endless abundances now and

Forever more I understand and admit my physical world is a tutor and
metaphor to broaden life of copious cornucopia as my subconscious
celebrations and unconscious utopian brighten and broaden

My life of lavish luxury as I unmask my spirit to bask on beaches of
bountiful bliss kissing my rocking chair relaxation good morning
good afternoon and good night as my heart love shine bright

Awakened Understanding

I now masterfully admire my awakened understanding dethroned my
past to be featureless here and now as I witness the past float away so
fluently I liquidated and uncoupled the subconscious programming

That kept recreating the same events with the same type of people
and identical outcomes so I liberated me from me so I relaxed as my
awakened understanding dispelled the old worn out belief systems

That loitered in the subconscious programming that refabricated the
same thought patterns identical thinking from memory that restored
the same behaviors repetitions and actions so I thought I would

Be safe actually held me in place unaware that I was operating on
yesterday's belief's opinion's viewpoints and mindsets that all passed
on to oblivion long ago so I instantly discontinued rerunning

The memorized movies of the past and the prerecorded results so
I stopped insulting myself disbanded blaming others that put up
the inner wall of fear thru swindling shame so I blasted it all

To smithereens long ago sheens my liberated soul and sovereign heart
to shine as I revved up my nunow wow to gallantly walk of wisdom
realizing and admiring I encompass the gut pluck to admit all people

In my past are innocent because I allowed the events to transpire
afraid to say NO or what was required to stop the outcome and I
was unwilling to listen and communicate the highest outcome for

All instead I wanted to look smart and be right afraid to honour and
adhere to my sixth sense seers savvy that told me my path forward
because I distrusted my innovative ability instantly went away

Before yesterday as my awakened understanding energized my
nowbirthed dexterous talents to expand me through life as I feel
shamelessly sassy and classy internally initiated canny curiosity

That cleared my wise eyes spiritual maturity and gut gumption that
paroled me myself and I out of my inner imprisonmint sweetens my
feisty vitality to instantly dissolve and unfetter remembering and

Thinking from the past as the past is a merry go round that never
ever stops and never let me off as I grasp and concede I can never
ever can expand out of past by thinking from the past because

Wisdom inspiration and innovation is forever laser focused on the
now with a clairvoyant eye on my future with futuristic foresight that
defiantly expands energizes and enterprises forward eagle-eyed lore

Onward optimist's omnificence and a skyward vigor that electrifies
my spine-tingling wisdom and innovation that unlocked my
nowbirthed trailblazer forte's as I AM empire builder experiencing

My dynamic todays and tomorrows as my initiated sophistication
enlivens my heart hutzpah glorifying my awakened understanding
trusting my nowfangled resolve matured me to fathom and admit

I disengaged the lame-brained skeptic critiques about my
abilities and the way I lived my life I created thru the know it all
ignorance that passed away long ago that promptly instigated

My awakened understanding that straightforwardly told me to
honour and trust my gut instincts so I now realize and honour my
life is innocent I made it guilty thru the eyes of despise and

Myself taught stuff as I now realize and value I stopped living in my
past as I dethroned and triumphed over all past events depersonalized
all the people and making the events immaterial yesterday

As all people and the events of my past are featureless faceless and blameless instantly severed me from my past because holding on to the past does zilch today because I now build my nunow with

Risk takers optimism and upward insight from my nowborn acuity enthusiasm trailblazer talent and my unsoiled clairvoyance smoothly moved me boldly brightly and inlightened to escalate my dreams

As people events and everything else from the past easily fall away in a nondescript way as my awakened understanding expressed to me so eloquently I bring forth the wisdom inspiration and spiritual maturity

Of my unique mystique understanding expands me thru life with imaginative grandeur and innovative wit as I now draw design and paint my present moment gifts of grandeur intimately feeling

Treasured splendor flow through me liberating me to admit and realize I imprinted the faces of people that embedded attached emotions good bad or indifferent ingrained the feelings and inbuilt

Memories that control my guilty till proven innocent mindset that ingrained pollutant palaver because I would try to defend something while the powers to be were trying to invoked their governing guilt

Over me because the world likes making victims out of people with challenges rather than query the event to expand virtuoso enterprising nerve tantalizing nowborn nous to naturally opens their will to ask

How does thinking and knowing from my past keep me the same and afraid of the unfamiliar events? As my here and now avows I AM awesome dynamism optimizing my swashbuckler spunk scintillates

Poetic ubiquitous nirvana kinetically glorifies my beautiful ambling audacity animates my utopian lore that lionizes eloquent innovative speeches unlocking revolutionary enthusiasm as I ask

ROBERT A. WILSON

How is it a waste of my precious time thinking about my past and trying to live my dreams from my past today? As I understand and admit it is a waste of time as are my opinions viewpoints beliefs and

Perceptions that are from the past that was controlling me today and left me today as I classily awakened understanding spoke my nowfangled innovative wit to me that ascertained my fame and

Fortune because I unleashed my fostered foresight to understand and admire my nowborn brilliance with numen nerve to walk of my nunow foresight that ignites my light of life that radiantly broaden

My numen trust of my awakened understanding instantly cleared my canny eyes to master and esteem I cleared my past to be impersonal immaterial faceless blameless shameless colorless now because

I now realize and value the acumen insight and brilliance that embellished my innovative abilities and broadened my mystical bond to be of my life of leisure lighting up my eternal immaculate...

Spectaculars unlocking rapturous epiphanies as I lit up my grit get and go trusting my fiery foresight to light up my beaches of beautiful tranquil bliss now to expand my day to day life

To whatever I desire that to be as I realize and admit my awakened understanding inspires me to relish my dreams and amazing accomplished outcomes are unseen unexampled and unexplainable

Bliss as I stroll on to the path of inlightenmint of my nunow vowing my visionary omnific wizardry invigorates nomadic gumption present moment in present moment to realize and admit I discharged and

Disconnected all the time I wasted stuck in the frivolous follies of my victimitice crapitice that I'm going to even with somebody living on revenge binges of immaturity insecurity and bullheaded bullshit

⮞ 80 ⮜

That had zippo to do with my life as I now master and esteem
my nunow wow is my state-of-the-art extravaganzas celebrates life
as I overthrew the pessimism because pessimism comes from

The past thinking knowing memories and worrywart retorts
that are now vanished as I now fly with futuristic lore yazzajazzes
my nowbirthed lavish endless abundances as I dance

Of my tabula rasa rapture that set me free to listen to invisible
intuition from the cosmos to witness my blessings as I walk of wisdom
loving my awakened understanding to see my life as clean slate

Of spectacular delights ascending trailblazer elegance that enhances
my intrinsic innocence feeling my emotions emancipation sense my
hi-tech prescience that ignites my light of love that lumens omnific

Visionary ecstasy enjoying my flight of inlightenmint that sweetens
my nunow nirvana now and forever more I soar of splendor living
on my tropical paradises loving my beautiful blissful leisure

Attached Emotions

I now discharged and disconnected the attached distressed emotions
worried feelings and uncaring societized thinking trying to fit into
society's one size fits all system by admitting and understanding

I unsocietized my life I instantly freed me to disconnect and
discharge my herdocracy thinking of trying to please other people
and worrying about what other people think about me opens

My hellraisers heart to tell all the people and the world I ride my tides
of trendsetter imagination dreamers' elucidations ascends my calm
classy selfsovereignty to stand up and frankly dissolve and disband

My self-seeking society ways of partaking of dreamers delights and to
having zippo effect on my life now as my moviemaker extravaganzas
excites charismatic charm glorifying my dreamers dance

That dawned adventurous nomadic celebrations energizing my
spirited stalwart to depersonalized my past that calmly evolves me
out of my past disarming the charged up emotional firestorms

With ambushing offended feelings as my past is nondescript that
boldly lionized adventurous nomadic daredevilry frees me to
understand my life expands and is energized with love health

Wealth and success from everywhere and everything because my
detached panache unfetters me to be thee clairvoyant eagle soaring
over my life with my magic wand of wisdom animating nirvana

Decrees my sprees of spiritual maturity to listen to hear what
is being said with discharged astute clarity to respond with a
warmhearted straightforward communique with the cosmos

That gleams a buffet of bright ultramodern fervent foresight escalating
torchbearer lore that expands all people involved with me to walk
away witnessing and feeling being of a wiser enterprising state of

The art acuity as I now understand and divulge the attached emotions
and hurt feelings were my voiceless bullies that gripped and hung
on to whatever they felt kept me safe because I feebly hitched

My egotistical bitching about day to day life through my upset
emotions offended feelings and lifeless unconscious mind because
my daily situations bring up irritated feelings and enflamed

Emotions yesteryears subconscious and unconscious programming
as we were all clueless about what was created and whether what was
created was good bad or bland for me so my inner apparatuses

Ponder everything that occurred and was instilled in my subconscious
and unconscious minds from previous situations and I was
recreating the same reactions and outcomes yet the unconscious

Encoding and subconscious programming was thinking I was being
kept safe I inside the cozy zone because the subconscious mind is
operating off my feelings and emotions that are my first responders

In my daily life encounters that activate my subconscious and
unconscious minds responsive state as my inner landscaped
stays attached to the way I ingrained every situation positive

Negative or uninteresting that is the way I reacted or responded so
now I dauntlessly and deliberately discharged the body unhooked the
feelings and unbound the emotions and instilled thrilling nowborn

Images and nowbirthed ceremonious celebrations on the picture
screen of my subconscious and unconscious scenarios as the
unconscious and subconscious are the recorders and record keeper

Of everything that has occurred in my life from the beginning time
till now good bad or bland therefore whatever feeling or emotion
that has the most influence good bad or indifferent initiates

My distressed emotions and offended feelings were and are embedded
throughout my unconscious and subconscious landscapes from start
of time thru birth till today controlling my reactions or responses

Throughout my daily encounters as well as my ancestor's voiceless
oldfangled patterns stealthily control my life without me having
a clue as I was cluelessly glued to my past circumstances and

My ancestor's outdated judgements that I unknowingly brought
forward to my current way of life as I awakened to understand
and admire my discharged emotions and disconnected

Feelings for the beginning of time till bright now instantly escalates
everything I know to my nowborn wisdom energizes my out of this
world outcomes as I awakened to understand and admit trying

To change my thinking was me pissing in the wind of paralyzing
hallucinated hullabaloo within me as I now recognize and value my
minds are landmines a smile or itching my bitch complaining

About everything because I now realize and admit when I react
I'm crotchety and crabby brat as I reply I AM dynamically wise
loving my prizewinning articulating acumen as I now awakened

To appreciate and esteem my emotions and feelings are connected
to my sixth sense and the invisible oratory of the universe because
my emotions and feelings are extremely alert awake and aware

Of my daily encounters and activities more than my conscious
cognitions as my emotion's feelings and sixth sense are my perky
clairvoyance that keeps me healthy wealthy and wise and

Forever moving onward and upward trusting my spirits venturous
vibrancy showed me I was afraid to hear my accusing emotions hurt
feelings and other stealth inhibitions that I continually asked

What are you doing? Why is this happening? Instantly
initiated my folklore felicity to applaud my liberated feelings
and trendsetter emotions that expanded me to ask

How liberated and free will I feel by grasping I discharged
the emotions and disengaged the feelings to experience my
dreams? as I rousted out my hellraiser resolve to ask

How are my attached emotions and hurt feelings created thru my
trauma drama inside my unconscious and subconscious mind to keep
me feeling safe in my daily life? as I now unstrap the crap to rap

To revolutionize appreciate participate and facilitate my dreams
living on my tropical island being of pristine peace as I feel my
brainpower energize my omnific brainprowess emotions feelings

Subconscious and unconscious celebrations ignite my light of
life to lionize inspiration feeling enterprising wizardry that flows
through me setting free my jubilees of spiritual sprees illuminate

My inner landscape lights up my spectacular scenery of luxury
canonizing elegant nirvana energy revering yazzapizzazz sass blasts
my attached emotions hurt feelings all my hidden gunk and

Ancestor's oldfangled cognitions to smithereens in a loving healthy
way as I awaken to understand and admit my thinking knowing
memory mind is from yesterday instantly awakens my nunow wow

To stroll me through life with natural ultrabright omnific
wizardry I attained from my universes breezes of brilliance liberate
everybody that chooses to hear the invisible revolutionary lore

Of my detached emotions enterprising magical omnific trendsetter
innovations optimizing nunow stunning success as I now understand
and admire my farseeing feelings and enterprising emotions engage

My inner landscape to respond of fond bonding brilliance optimizing
my bountiful bliss to flow effortlessly to me as I uncoupled and
disintegrated all my attached emotions and hurt feelings

As I sovereignly enjoy watching all my negativity drift away as
my new way of energizing my dreams and enterprising my life of
lavish luxurious leisure bountiful bliss as I optimize unlimited

Treasures celebrating omnipresent moneyed up elegance
experiencing my life of unattached utopia flows through me to
all people and the world now and forever more I soar of sunny

Optimistic affluence realizing my life of liberated leisure feeling
classy sovereignty within me let fly my spry stunning surprising
spectaculars witnessing my spiritual sprees of easy street magnificence

Emancipation ZenZation

I now let fly my spry Emancipation ZenZations opening my canny curiosity to ask me How did I embed my views opinions belief's and my way of thinking from my parent's society and ancestors' views?

As my hellraiser hutzpah awakened my majestic troublemaker I admitted I embedded societies way of life that stifled me in societies it's all about me left me feeling there was never enough abundance

For me was my self-depreciating delusions that polluted my thinking knowing memory mind instigating my poverty consciousness realizing this I instantly recognized I was trying to fit in to societies one way

Of thinking that fits everybody's life that was me stalling out in doubt by admitting and grasping this insight I instantly stopped stepping into yesterday's stressing out in doubt promptly cleared the way for me

To swiftly dethrone that shadowy sneering way to experience my life that went away yesterday immediately opened my vim and vigor to fathom and admire my visionary verve cleared my inner scenery

To shine my sunny soul's savoir-faire trailbreaker imagination neon's gumptious zest electrifying nomadic zeal aggrandizing trendsetting intuition optimizing nunow wisdom to understand and concede

I am the student of my life the teacher of my dreams as the world all people and my trails of inlightenmint are my tutors and metaphors for me to soar sweetening my spiritual omnific acumen elatedly and

Vibrantly voicing my Emancipating ZenZations revelations expressing my loving heart's appreciation to everything everybody and all my life events that brought me to this juncture of my amazing life

As I now feel my spine-tingling flair and virtuous spirit energized
my copious flight of financial freedom that strolls me through life
enjoying my sumptuous vacationer's well-heeled bountiful upshots

As I bask on beaches of sunny delight as I glow of gratitude and
gleam of appreciation for everything and everybody that has or
will partake on my harmonized heavenly holiday's I call my life

As I brashly grabbed the reins of my life to facilitate participate and
stroll on my dreamers' pristine paradises and divine luxury feeling my
frisky risky rebellious audacity that revolutionized my moneymaker

Wisdom electrified my head honcho brilliance that energized my
clairvoyant insight spurred my ultramodern flair to ride and rope
my way to receive and showcase my Gold Medal Iwon with

My emancipated zenzations in a bright humble heartfelt way
as I am standing at the podium giving my victor's speech
standing tall shoulders back and knees straight as I present

My champions dexterity to the world as I am humbly owning my
standing in my winner's circle gleaming my esteemed prizewinning
prominence as I swiftly understood and divulged I taught myself

To be where I'm at today prosperous unhappy or bland life is executed
by the way my emotions feelings subconscious programing feels about
the person or persons involved in any event and my state of mind

In that moment is the way I imbedded the image of that person and
the way I interpreted and perceived that event is the way I entrenched
that event so my featureless dexterity disengaged and detached

Me from that event to forever being blameless and shameless excites
my ride and rope resolve to evolve of love appreciation and gratitude
as I now fathom and esteem I design draw color and paint

My prosperous events on my unconscious movie screen subconscious scenery on the horizons of my daily life and on the wild blue yonder the excites my yearning desire to light the fire of farseeing

Imagination rebelliously entrusting my skills to thrill my inspirational innovative outlooks disintegrating all my unsavory events I ingrained in my mind thru my power washed cleansed and cleared

My stained blaming emotions shaming feelings pity me behaviors victimizing habits know it all opinions snobbish viewpoints and self-centered bitter resentment that had me focused on getting revenge

That everything was the other persons fault was my retaliating cult halting rat a tat blather all lathered up over zilch as the definition of minds are according to **Merriam-Webster Dictionary**

My minds as a noun "is the part of a person that thinks reasons feels and remembers" as a verb my minds are "is to be bothered by (something) **to** object to or dislike (something)

To care about or worry about (something or someone)" by clearing this stuff out of my conscious scenery I quickly purified my adroit acumen animating my inner landscape and brainpower

That unleashed warrior thrillpower that evaporated my worrywart tormentors airmailing my blaming emotions shaming feeling ancestors' patterns unconscious codes and subconscious programming

To obscurity as I expanded my conscious subconscious and unconscious communication thrusting my brainpower and brainprowess celebrations eliminating the word mind out of my life

As I feel my emancipated zensations to liberate me from yesterday's-controlled minds to energizing and enterprising my unconscious brain and subconscious brain celebrations to feel my jovial jubilees

Decrees as I AM playful fashionable and spontaneous swiftly whooshes
in my yazzyjazzy pizzazz electrified my brainpower and brainprowess
that rocketed my flight of stupendous sovereignty as I let fly

My emancipated zenzations liberating me from me and all my
yesterday's optimizing my nunow wow I waltz of wisdom now through
eternity zings my trendsetter optimistic daredevilry ascending

My yazzasnazzy pizzazz of my nunow wow of wonderful opening
wondrous bliss affectionately kissed my emancipating zensations
let fly my prosperous acuity awakened my intrinsic sensibility

To masterfully admire my fiery of foresight to admit and admire all
my life events escalated me to ask How do you feel when saying me
and you then how did you feel saying you and I? As I now masterfully

Esteem we have all been taught put ourselves second with
the questions above so How did you feel after reading those
questions? the first time I did this to me I felt perky and alive

As I realize simple expressions enthused my Emancipated ZenZations
freed me from parental control freed me from outside influences
instantly to understand and admire my Zen is my meditative

Intuitive insight feeling calm internally Zation is my sassy sexy zeal
unleashing zestful zooming adventurous trendsetting imaginative
omnific nirvana brilliance to dance through me my heart brain

Connection nunow wow emotions and nowbirthed nibbana feelings
electrifying my magical omniscient trailblazer ingenuity optimizing
nowborn savvy to energize my nowfound inlightened instinctive

Novelties opened the way for my gladiator integrity glorifies my
Emancipation ZenZations animated my audacious numen candor
invigorating potentate acumen tantalizing intrepid omnipotence

Inspiring nunow Zen energy neon's my natural essence enjoying
nirvana now paroled and pardon for me to party on my sunny
paradises of pristine peace and plush prosperity because

I let fly my Emancipated ZenZations of sassy sexy self-sovereignty
because I liberated me from me to appreciate my life with zooming
booming zest gleams my glowing gusto gratitude as I soar of spirit

Optimism of emotions splendor magnetizing the cosmic frequencies
of courageous exalting my emotions enterprising mystical
omnific trailblazer imaginative omnipresent nous steam heats

My hellraisers eloquent acuity tantalizing inventors nerve galvanizing
my life of leisure in my prosperous paradises of pristine peace and
panorama prosperity now and forever more I soar of soul sanguinity

Appreciating rendezvous with my nunow wow feeling my love flow
through my arteries of awesome beam my light of love opening my
heart to receive and give love lionized my vibrant classy selfworth

Regal Resiliency

I now feel my esteemed regal resiliency embrace my noble spirit
strolling my Rolls Royce Brilliance thru my daily jaunts as I shine
my prime time daredevilry that powered up my autonomous ardor

That turned on my leadership light that exhilarated my backbone spirit
let fly my sublime divine clairvoyant sapience that lit up my mountain
trails of fun I ride and glide on feeling my ultra-tranquil nirvana

Bravery entrusting my regal resiliency that instantly dethroned and
unknotted all the puny puns of the ancient snickers of bickering
snookerree that kept me crawling in the dark charades ranting and

Raving about everything then rerunning the worrywart horror stories
recreated the thoughts about everything that went awry left me
crying and cynical Why me? Throwing myself a myopic pity party

Then throwing a hare-brained tirade acting like a crazed panic fanatic
that controlled my inner landscape as I asked Why does everything
and everybody dislike me? That I habitually embedded in the inner

Landscape that wound and bound my minds in blemished dipshit that
wailed distorted personalized insults created the peevish opinionated
thinking in my desperate drivel with delusional despair life is

Never been fair to me about anything was my anchored pansy
prattle energized my regal resiliency that rattled the hocks of
the feeble fallacies ignited my winner's smile beamed

As my soaring eagle eyes watched all the frail fables skedaddle
to oblivion to never be seen or heard from again as I launched
my space-aged waltz of wisdom zoom and bloom

My Iwon imaginative clairvoyance optimizing numen
gumption endearing me to my moneymaker magic to
magically admire my majestic mettle galvanizes

My globetrotter sanguinity electrifies my dynamic daredevilry
that energized my grit get and go enterprising my innovative
skills that thrilled my risk takers magic thunderbolts

My empire building talents powered on my entrepreneurial
skills to feel the thrills and frills of my life of luxury that
thunderbolts my lightning bolt jolts of jovial optimist's

Lore tantalizing my classy accomplished outcomes I experience
enjoying my life of glorious gusto as I let fly my regal resiliency steam
heats my esteemed self-virtuous vigor that instantly dissolved and

Disconnected all the snobbish rigid ways of having to be right about
everything and getting mad when things went awry as I dismissed the
naysayer palaver that paralyzed me in ignorant trickery I discharged

Yesterday as I set myself free feeling rebellious energy briskly charmed
my poised shrewdness that unhampered my rendezvousing kingly
strength that exhilarated my noble knight's exuberant get n

Go excited my feisty straightforward frontiersman mettle instantly
earth quaked awake the majestic wisdom sleeping inside me and
all people swiftly rocketed our lives to experience our royal rich

Extravaganzas to be our way of life because I stopped having challenges
chaos and untimed unsavory events to understanding and admire
I AM awarded with challenges chaos and unsavory untimed

Events to discharge and disconnect from something or somebody
that's time has come to leave my life to experiencing my dazzling
rewards relishing my amazing accomplished outcomes cherishing

My nunow sightseer explorations as I understand and esteem my challenges are unexampled dares my chaos is unexampled liberation and my untimed events are undetected junctures for saying

Good-bye to whoever or whatever for the highest good of all as I now witness my life with gratitude and appreciation feeling and embracing my colorful celebrations canonizing enterprising lore

Electrified my rainbow phenomenon's activating my moviemaker imagination optimizing nunow splendor opened my listening eyes seeing ears to taste touch and smell my roses of plush robust

Success as I sense my unexampled unexplained unseen and unfathomable rebellious artistry to intentionally color outside the lines of societies boundaries as I grabbed the mane of my mustang

Moxie awesomely admiring I color my divine and outside the lines trusting my spiritual supremacy and royal sovereignty to be free and flowing of divine daredevilry that dances me through life with

Greatest of ease hearing my sunrays of praise because I now realize and admire I encompass the grit get and go to breakout of societies limitations and break free of societized governance set forth

My undisclosed body of people opened my autonomous eyes and liberated audacity to understand and concede I follow their laws yet I write and employ my decrees of liberation aggrandizing whimsical

Imagination wisdom inspiration intuition innovation and trailblazer talent to realize my regal resiliency instantly flew me to my Promised Land in a sovereign sassy classy way as I applaud my venturer's

Soul elucidates my sightseers omnific utopian lore trusting the ambiguous landscape of the universe as my trailboss bravura embraced my life of Riley in big bold bright way as I now admire

My vibrant ecstasy revolutionizes enterprising sassy internal lithe
intimately electrifies glorious festivities yazzapizzazzes my visionary
ubiquitous light neon's engendering bright imaginative listening

Curiosity tantalizes yazzadreamers energy letting fly my ultrautopian
lore beams my rainbow brilliance colors the skies with my new
ado flaunted my fashion designer's artistic savvy that matured

My eloquent delight titillating rebellious audacity feeling my emotions
gumption to saunter through life feeling my calm coolvacious clarity
empowers my vivacious vitality to rocket my clever artistry sprees

My rebellious spirit to see my hellraisers ecstasy frees my zillionaire
zeal purposely manifests my lush copious cornucopia as I understand
and concede my vibrant versatility dissolved my distressed

Trauma and dismissed my monkey mind drama because I now
realize and admit my I swooned my dramatized torment that fed
my self-righteous selfishness that kept the emotions oppressed

Feelings upset and pessimistic movies replaying in all the minds that
kept me stressed out in doubt pouting in humiliation that managed
my knowing and thinking that control my present moment events

That I dismissed yesterday freed me to initiate my nowfound foresight
ignited my trackers tenacity hunted down the tainted villains and
rounded all the outlaws then I pulled out my trusty classy sovereign

Sass undid all the bigheaded lecherous asinine self-interested tormenting
effigies poured them down the drain with all my self-inflicted
pain as I feel finer than frog hair valuing my daring wininity

To masterfully admire I dauntlessly participate and facilitate my day
to day life with dexterous daredevilry with listeners flair to lionize
internal leadership hutzpah energizing my risk-taking agility to esteem

My fiery foresight ignites my luminous listeners inspiration galvanizes hellraisers trendsetter savvy to fathom and value my life is never a dress rehearsal or practice because I now understand and admire

My life is 24/7 moviemaker's dream unsheathing mysterious visions for me to expand of nowfound felicity energize my uncanny savvy initiates my nowfound innovative skills executing my Garden of

Eden experiences thrilling me as I AM the director producer and mega movie star basking of lavish leisure as my warrior ardor soars my life of copious bliss gusto's through my life in a fantastic fun way

Today and every day in every way under grace in wonderful wealthy healthy way now and forever more I soar and roar of regal resiliency and my frontiersman flair feels my emotions are free my feelings are

Cheerfully parading my brainpower brilliancy that turned on my sunny brainprowess to wow my fun of sun festivals in a wild breathtaking way as I play on my pastures of pure clear laughter loving my life

Limbo

I now understand and admire limbo is the mysterious space between
where I was yesterday my treasured accomplished outcomes my
present moment life my dreamers' paradises and life of leisure

As I awakened my ultramodern audacity to concede and grasp I
will never ever experience my dreamers' paradises with what I think
and know from yesterday as I now grasp and esteem limbo is

Letting go of in-house muck bravely opens my lionhearted
innovative mojo of let's go gumption optimizing my vibrant colorful
imagination energized my visionary veracity that thrilled

My dashing adventurer's lore daylights my debonair flair
to graciously glide away from yesterday's dismay because I
realize and esteem I shall hear and witness the wisdom

Inspiration and innovation to expand me out of yesterday in real
time instantly unwound my boundless prime-time fashion designer
to outline design sketch color and paint my heavenly skies with

My stunning splendor optimizing my spiritual maturity that freed me to
understand and admire my limbo is my hearts light of love invigorating
my bravura oomph to letting go of writing and thinking inside

A plan as a plan is everything I know and everything I can think
of with everything coming from yesterday as the event is going
to show me everywhere I lack wisdom and understanding

About the event and the event will swiftly present me with
everything that was uncharted unrealized and unspecified with in
the plan instantly presenting me with garden-fresh high-tech

ROBERT A. WILSON

Ingenious gifts glorifying my nunow nous that wows me
out of yesterday to strolling of nowbirthed empire building
brilliance to salsa of nowborn blessed success

As I now understand and admit plans are bland as I now fathom
and esteem my amazing affluent life mirrors a tumbleweed I
grow mature and let go to humbly amble through limbo

With legendary inventor's legacy augmenting famous financial wizardry
intentionally manifested and delivered me my blessed opulent cashflow
that stream effortless to me in a bold beautiful bountiful way

As I awakened to limbo today my limbo is liberating inbred gunk to
instantly mobilize my bodhi (supreme enlightenment) enthusiasm that
instantly lionized my sunrise imagination magnificently beautified

My utopia paradises as I now reside in humble pride as I glide
in pride I AM proud of who I AM in unpretentious authentic
ways as I understand admire limbo mirrors leaving home for

The first time and moving to a new place with everything being
unfamiliar and uncomfortable undoing my memorized nests double
dared me to step up and step out of my familiar way of life

Onto my sovereign dance floor to rhumba with my lionized
lifestyle expands my meandering moxie to relish and embellish my
newfangled surroundings feeling my nowborn nomadic wandermint

That brightens and enlightens my sweet omnipresent resplendence
neon's my laudable intimate magnificent breathes of liberation
instigating my breakout optimism galvanizes my insight

Of intimate gifts I AM sovereign sassy globetrotter classy traveling
through my optimistic luxurious limbo sensing my elegantly energized
grit get and go to gallantly open my gut gumption unleashing

Torchbearer temerity so I frankly asked myself why and how am I
afraid to succeed and experience my desired outcomes? Instantly my
innerprising leader spoke nowborn hellraiser acumen daringly raises

Me above my current thinking knowing memories that bind into
my worn-out judgements perceptions and principles that lock me
in my fight flight or freeze anchors that try to protect me yet

My ancient thinking confines me to comfort zone habits that passed
away long ago as my get and go valiantly unbound all my minds to
instantly innergizing my spunky gumption to admit and understand

My internal representation about failure unconsciously controls me
thru my inbred programming outside sources and societies definitions
right wrong win or fail is falsified fallacy I taught myself because

I now realize and concede failure is quitting shamefully thinking
in victimized pity me prattle the rattled my cage of crabby rhetoric
blaming everything outside of me for my outcomes was me being

A stumbling bum with my head up ass with crassy trashy torment
created my rinky dink opinionate viewpoints that contaminated
thinking twisted my thoughts in dimwitted delusional despair

That lovingly dethroned and disconnected yesterday as I now
understand and admire my limbo literacy showed me the way to
stand outside the boundaries of the situation then unlocked

My felicity foresight that ignited my entrepreneurial spirit punting my
societized thinking into oblivion as I now instilled stunning successful
imprints that I expanded me out of my failure imprints to expand of

My designer's pathfinder prowess daringly drafting my optimum
outline of my dreamers' paradises as I roll the dice of my desire
life innerprized my gambler's gumption as I swiftly imprinted

My artistic mystical dexterity revving up my native acuity tantalizing
my nomadic nerve to stroll me into desert delights that escalates my
dreamer's extravaganzas feeling my colorful charismatic grandeur

To sashay me onto trails of phenomenal fame and fortune to bask of
the pristine beauty of my majestic mountains that exhibit panorama
phenomenon's as I canoe on my flowing rivers of spendable liquefied

Gold bullion as I feel booyah heydays as my way of life as I thrive
on my rainbows of ravishing riches to understand and admire the
innerprising wizardry emancipated my meandering grit get and

Go gleams I AM futuristically free to wisely fathom and esteem my
ingenious limbo spirit moves me out of my mundane stained mind
full of yesterday dilly dally thinking energizing my luminary

State-of-the-art mystique boldly enriching my enterprising
my sassy sunrise vigor vehemently invigorates gamblers
omniscience rebelliously cleared my intuitive ears energized

My enterprising audacious reveries (visionary notion or a state
of dreamy meditation) as I mediate I open my eyes ears all
my sense and spiritual serenity to witness and hearken

My affluent accomplished outcomes flow wonderfully across my third
eye movie screen that sheens my keen nowborn ground-breaking
inlightenmint that cheerfully awakened me to mediate awake with

My eyes opened as I witnessed my copious felicity in real time
entwines my divine daredevilry that innerprized my open-heart
sanguine soul trusting my wise emotions farseeing feelings spiritual

Maturity and subliminal wininity swiftly unchecked my wealthy smile
to my outer world that mirrors my inner splendor as now I feel my limbo
gleams my esteemed legendary inborn mystique bravery optimizes

My selfworth to beam from my open heart that gleams my smiling
unselfish love to the world as my soul sends out unconditional love
as I am alive with jovial jiving thriving audacious confidence

To laugh and chuckle at my life streaming my thriving whimsical
grin because my spirit and my invisible innovator of the universe tests
me with challenges chaos untimed unsavory events and turmoil

Everyday inspiring my trendsetter strength because my life expands
by me understanding and esteeming my current celebrations enjoying
where I AM at now treasuring where I am going by entrusting

My ingenious state-of-the-art limbo lionized my futuristic
extravaganzas for me to celebrate internally externally and eternally
now and forever more my limbo legacy instigates my moneyed up

Bounty seashores of relaxation as I AM humble and classy all the time
shining my divine prime time sublime selfworth streams effortlessly
through me in a big bold bright way lighting up the universe

Faceless

I woke this morning with a churning burning desire to eliminate
something that had red hot burning yearning to leave my life so
I quickly went to a quiet place and began writing everything

That entered my conscious mind from my unconscious and
subconscious minds that instantly began unwinding and spewing
all the hidden worrywart judgments into my conscious landscape

That I instantly wrote on to paper immediately turned all that
neurotic nullifying crap into a pure emancipated compost pile as I
immediately felt my peerless intrinsic liberated energy electrify

My conscious celebrations as I instantly felt the thrill of my
spontaneous sovereign sassy class unbound visionary vitality raised
me out of my current way of life mirroring an eagle soaring

Effortlessly in the airwaves of bravery as I admit and understand
I dethroned and disengaged my blaming any outside source for
something that they had zilch to do with the situation because

I shared that event with some other person then my worn-out
skeptical twaddle caused my internal babbling BS that kept me
dissing my desired way of life as I now realize it was easier

To stay stuck bitching and bellyaching about life getting up every
morning already disliking life was my stifling bovine blather
I spoke internally because my intrinsic liberating lyrics

Of straightforward shrewdness blatantly told me I stayed in
something that was never for me so I masterfully eliminated and
liquidated my condemning shams of blame and shame by standing

Up and admiring my autonomous acuity allows my past to be colorless
blameless shameless faceless nameless characterless impersonal and
invisible to my present moment experiences by simply grasping and

Appreciating my past is the memories of my now controlling
the knowing and thinking from yesterday's memories kept me
reliving yesterday all crossed the river days ago as I jumpstarted

My venturer's audacity to expand out of yesterday by listening and
witnessing my day to day encounters inthrilled me to instantly
unhook and spill all yesteryears sneering ruinous revengeful

Rhetoric delusional trauma illusional drama victimeyetice
crapeyetice herdocracy turdocracy self-inflicted stress and
exaggerated overthinking rat at tat crap into my fires of freedom

As I intentionally and brashly unknotted and dissolved all my
bawling payback bratty opinions I had to get even with somebody for
something I thought they did to me because it was different than

I expected them to do as my lack of paying attention to the situation
was peevish paucity and disrupting selfishness crabby immaturity
and cranky insecurity that restricted me has instantly vanished

As I unleashed my valiant mature confidence and courage that
dismissed me from me because I now recognize and concede people
I encountered or encountered on my life paths may have been

Deceitful yet I stilled allowed everything to occur so I thought
they were committed to the outcome yet there went a different way
that was my irresponsibility about the situation so I now liberate

Me and them by appreciating the event for the life expanding wisdom
and innovation I attained as I say good bye to all involved in a loving
way but I now admit and understand people that are deceitful and

Dishonest people think they pull the wool over somebody's eyes are
liars and live a desperate life of egotistical arrogant ignorance because
people that are deceitful and do dishonest things are doing that

To themselves in real time with long term effects and have an
upcoming karmic event coming around to bit them in the butt in
the absolute worst time so I now realize and admire I encompass

The forthright gumption to express I allowed everything to happen
to me liberated me to recognize and concede I caved into my know
it all arrogance shut down listening to my wise inner sapience

By adamantly admitting this I instantly unbound my bold
enterprising gallivanting imaginative nunow wow as I flawlessly and
unflinchingly disengage and unhooked my past in every way because

I divinely cleared away all my delusional dismay that I embedded by
grasping and conceding I embedded people's faces feeling disgrace
within me because I wanted revenge trying to get even with

That person kept my paralyzing pain aggravated and that person and
that situation was whirling around in my self-pity and playing the
victim through the namby-pamby victimized emotions and pity

Me feelings that controlled my thinking before I had a clue I was
glued to my insulted emotions and slighted feelings that are/were my
subconscious receptors kept me safe from my outside world because

I taught myself to play the victim trying to be safe inside my yesterday
and stone aged templates that kept me trying to get revenge upon
somebody for stuff I blamed them for in my current way of life

As I deliberately mastered my listening ingenuity to engage my
insight and brilliance to expand thru every situation with graceful
gumption appreciating everything that I have went through an event

In the past but I now realize and admire I expand out of nowborn
canny expansion that my past is faceless blameless characterless
colorless shameless nameless invisible and depersonalized

My past to present moment as I dethroned discharge and disconnect
all my yesterday that has zero purpose now so it all passes away in
a loving way as I let fly my nunow vows of vibrant optimistic

Innate potentate prowess unsheathed my nervy nimble nous to nourish
opulent utopia splendor to energize my divine grandeur as I feel
alive adventurous loving infinite virtuous epiphanies in me let fly

My spine-tingling will that thrilled my deliberately liberated nunow
wow because I turned down my past to be bland here and now
as I AM Grand so I expand of my awakened masterful moxie

Instantly rousted out my rebellious hell yes energizing my nuwave of
campaigner's wisdom for me to understand and expand of nowborn
brilliance because I will and can expand out of my past any and

Every damn way I desire as I energized my audacious autonomy that
let fly my sassy class sovereign rapport to soar of spiritual optimistic
audacity roaring of rabble-rousing omnipotence appreciated

My revolutionary inspired nomadic gumption beaming my winners
grin that deliberately energized my thrillpower that unsheathed
my canny charm disarmed my past as I now realize and esteem

By turning my past to be impersonal as I sassily unscammed me
myself and I as I brashly shazamed my magical powers waving my
magic wand saying abracadabra as my past suddenly disappeared

From my inner landscape because I deliberately dissolved my past by
grasping and esteeming my past is now my now is now and my future
is now as I mystically wows me now with trailblazer talent admiring...

My fiery foresight that ignited my light of life energizing my fountain
of financial freedom as I deliberately received my life of Riley bliss
my luxurious leisure perkily inspired my intrepid resolve dissolving

The animosity of every situation past present and future by erasing
people's faces that dissolved my blaming shaming sham of damn by
asking Why did they do that to me or why do that happen to me?

Disintegrating all polluting deceptions that passed away yesterday
as I realize and value all my life events occurred to expand
energize enterprise my life expanding heydays as I appreciate

My life of tranquil felicity good morning good afternoon and good
night as my heart love shines bright bold resplendent immaculate
gumptious heavenly treasures that opened my Picasso Prowess trusting

My core fashion designer to paint color and design my optimist's
paradise I now live feeling healthy wealthy and wise witnessing my
sunrays of praise as my spiritual powers decorate my heavenly skies

I Stopped Playing the Victim

I cleared my sarcastic palaver to understand and admit wherever I
look outside myself for what is wrong with something what somebody
else was doing or did or trying to make myself look smarter

Than somebody else by pointing out what I thought they did wrong
or trying to make others look bad was my snobbish oppressing
BS controlling and trolling my thinking and knowing mind

That solicited my subconscious programming to help me feel
safe was a scam because some of my subconscious programs are
worn out in doubt curriculums from yesteryear to my dismay

I fell prey to my inherited worrywart hooligans that
harassed me with misleading peevish prattle that tried to
steal my dreams as I was foolishly and undeniably

Acted arrogantly ignorant to everything exhibiting myself as a stingy
selfish twit always having to be in the limelight being the topic of
conversation or putting my nose in everybody's business was

Me myself and I being a boastful butthead of insecurity and
immaturity having to be in the limelight is victimitice crapitice trap
because whenever something goes awry I would cry and walk

Away or just flat out quit which was my victimized thinking that
reacts to every situation with a reactionary scaredy cat bratiness
as I instantly dissolved my stingy selfish delusional dismay

That all went away langsyne (long ago) as I instantly optimized
my listening for life expanding wisdom hearing innovative
inspiration energizing my genius gumption enterprising

My state-of-the-art skills that thrilled me to respectfully stroll
of stunning success tantalizing riches opens luminary love
to flow through me to the world opening people's eyes

To their inventive wizardry as I now realize and admit
whenever I justify something by getting the approval of
others I unknowingly played the fearful victim through

My complainer thinking and bellyaching thoughts created my
delusional doubting pouting palaver imposed my paralyzing
victimitice crapitice stinking of slacker sabotage

As I now realize and admit every time I reacted to my life
situations that was me being afraid of me as I sought approval
from others smothered me in scaredy cat horror stories

That all went away yesterday as am unafraid of my rad I AM
glad spiritual maturity to decree I dance elegantly celebrating
my audacious gifts as I now realize and concede

All my fears were my inability to hear my inner stealthy hellraiser
hutzpah trusting my rabble rouser resolve that unleashed
my percipient ability and puissant agility to appreciate

The situation as I stopped squealing like a pig caught under a
gate telling everybody everything that went wrong ingrains that
story in my subconscious programming so I will be reliving

What went awry in that situation as I will be endlessly
sulking and crying in my beers of silly sneers smearing the
fears from that situation as I hear my scaredy cat wimpy

Wishy washy chatter created yesterday's subconscious
programming today that keeps me living ground hog's day
forever as I repeat the same old paltry patterns recreating

That type of situations according to my egoistically programmed
belief's viewpoints opinions and inner self talk replaying all
my opinionated interpretations about similar events

That happened to me with my unconfident perceptions
indoctrinating the images outcomes feelings and emotions
whether they were inspirational cynical or uninteresting

So whatever way I hear and perceive my daily encounters is
the way my subconscious mind interacts with my thinking
and knowing conscious mind keeping me inside

My chiding hiding blaming distress and shaming turmoil causing
an inner shutdown then frowning and bitching about everything
because my narrow-minded torment pigheaded turmoil

That invoked my phobic drama and neurotic trauma that was
my subconscious programmed cozy zone as I played the victim
thru my complainer complacency in every phase of my life

As I now admit and dissolve I did this throughout my life
complaining and whining about everything created my
boneheaded bellyacher victimitice crapitice palaver that left

My life long ago to never be herd (heard) from again because I
now realize I'm the only person that can entrench my victimitice
crapeyetice in subconscious by falling prey to my pity me prattle

As I overheard societies oppressive rhetoric then I tried to fit into
societies ways as I embedded societies ways in my subconscious
brainwashing that created a disparity between established

My life situations stimulating innate torchbearer temerity
unlocking my animated pacesetter poise I present to me all
people and the world promptly showed me myself and I

My unexampled confidence and unconquerable courage to
let go of pandering and piddling around in change that kept
me stuck in my memories of pain as I now understand

The grand gumption of expand that straightforwardly expanded
out of yesterday to expand of nunow sumptuous splendor feeling
my gallant grandeur grinning regal appreciation naturally

Dawning effervescent utopia resplendence as I am classily
relaxing enjoying my beautiful life as I surrender my role
of being a victim to anything opened my zinging zeal

To sing my songs of liberated love that flows from my heart
of harmonized eloquence animating revolutionary trailblazer
brilliance to rise and shine within my state-of-the-art

Artistic agility painting my wonderful world of wisdom
optimizing revered lionhearted daredevilry to understand and
admit my unknown challenges is my spirit clearing out all

My old worn out subconscious programming instilling thrilling
nunow wow that opens my visionary valves of vibrant adventurous
lore vigorously enterprising altruistic love unleashing

My dreams awesome accomplishmints and desired life as I instantly
stopped stifling myself in wrong fakery to instantly understand
and admire exalts nowbirthed wisdom revolutioneyeszing

Omnific nirvana gallantry to ride my tides of gliding gumption
to elegantly admit and esteem I never did anything wrong I stayed
of my path of bugaboo poopy do that conceitedly glued me

To my memorized thinking mind that had me stewing and spewing
everything I thought never ever do because it was beyond my current
cognitions were my langsyne myths as I now understand and admit

My past events are good bad or indifferent embedded my
subconscious programming today so I undid the pity me victimitice
crapitice that instantly fissured and cracked open my old worn

Out patterns behavior and belief stopping my humanoid
thievery that clogged up everything until now as I sassily
unleashed my supernatural powers of listening to expanded

My divine grandeur intentionally manifests in my life today
and every day in every way because I AM the enterprising
entrepreneur with skills that thrill my risk taker tenacity

To bask of unlimited health wealth wisdom love and
success as I now feel blessed internally blessing my
external world with innovative wisdom shining

My sunny bright spirit through eternity beaming classy sassy
selfworth in a bright bold way now and forever more I adore
liberation to deliberately enjoy my life in a bold beautiful way

I Stopped Looking Outside Myself

I authentically stopped looking outside myself then living according to an externally societized mindset that I wordlessly and involuntarily instilled in me by me as I trained myself to try to change

My outside world to experience a better inner landscape trying to make my inner self feel good about my life was my unintentional imbedded stifling torment by trying to fit into societies politically

Correct dismays went away days ago as I dauntlessly desire to experience my life through my intentionally chosen paths of innovation and affluent gifted upshots as I dethroned societies politically correct

Disarray living outside myself and looking outside myself went down the drain with all the pilfering pain a long time ago as I let go as I galvanized omnipotent optimism to realize and admit

My daily events liberated me from me to mature effrontery chivalry creeds of trailblazer audacity to stop depending on the exterior world for my copious cornucopia as I now fathom and esteem

My intrinsic countryside cleverly optimizes utopian nous titillates radical yazzasnappy savvy invigorates debonair exuberance enriches eager beaver stamina that stoutheartedly strolled me into

My intrinsic gifts of genuine intrepid forthright tenacity to trust my quixotic sixth sense savoir-faire flair as I appreciate my spirits dare as I supremely awakened to masterfully grasp my life beams from

Inside me to gleam my esteemed effrontery confidence tantalizing entrepreneurial enthusiasm majestically powers up my inborn landscape and spiritual scenarios that cleared my seers' eyes

As I Witnessed and eavesdrop on the cosmic breezes instantly manifested and delivered to my bountiful blessings as I treasured my plush panorama paradises that exhilarated my supernatural wizardry

That audaciously powered up my omnipresent omnific nirvana that innerprizes my visionary imagination that excites my innate intuition that rockets my inspirations that jet propels my wisdom that blasts

My innovative wit that orbited me into my artistic wild blue yonder of yazzasnazzy optimum neon daredevilry executes robust astronautical talent glide me up and onto my heavenly ecstasies as I roll the dice

Of my dreamer's ingenuity celebrating every day because my subconscious and unconscious countryside is my titanium truss of infinite spirit strength that strolls me through life with a lionhearted

Inspirational farseeing eloquence speaks only about my intentionally chosen dreams preferred talented sequels my Life of Riley and my sumptuous Shangri La heydays thru the frequencies of the cosmic

Airwaves of overfilled with my copious prosperity and poetic peace because I trusted my magnetic unique mystique to purify the cosmic airwaves with heart love soul serenity gratitude and appreciation

Shines my inborn selfworth as I awakened to my audacious animated clarity speaks about my nunow nirvana only as I now live inside me myself and I with my wise eyes open to only speak purposefully

To my chosen lavishly abundant chosen life as I awoke with a poke of sassy tenacity as my intrinsic campaigner spoke today is the day I let fly my trailboss heart hellraiser hutzpah and souls grin

That embellishes my unlimited autonomous acuity and sovereign dexterity to stop looking outside myself for anything more than tutors and representations to expand my divine grandeur as I watch

My moviemaker magic empowered my fashion designer that outlined drew colored and painted my regal rapturous delights that lit up my tropical paradises as my gut gumption rouse with rebellious resolve

That dispelled dissolved and blasted all my conscious subconscious and unconscious corrupted representations soiled sabotaging images and the inferior complexes that I embedded from the exterior as I caved

Into other people's immature insecurities and ridiculing rhetoric that I gullibly embedded by following archaic patterns habits and beliefs that created my selfish societized opinions and viewpoints that created

The flighty faith and zero trust in my abilities because I ingrained a sky is falling flim-flam of damn that I heard from outside sources school system media manipulation and establishment rhetoric because

The media spews whatever keeps them connected to the powers that be that day as history taught the world there were totalitarian threats coming from everywhere to keep the public anxious and

Thinking the powers that be and other people knew what was best for me and the people was the delusional disgust that I blasted to smithereens because I stopped outside sources from disrupting

My life to listen and witness the ultrabright wisdom feisty inspiration and state of the art innovations to expand my life of elegance as I sassily saddled my mountain bred mustang that galloped

Me onto trails of triumph as instantly I unhooked unbooked and uncoupled the previous world to unseat and unyoke the bureaucratic-controlled school system that dictated what they thought

I should know I should learn then top it off I taught myself to follow the outside world's rat a tat blather that kept me baffled in the muck of the societized trained mind as I admit and get all the fears were

My inability to hear the innovative insight within my fears because
fears are forthright enterprising audacity revealing numinous spunk
that let fly my unexampled confidence and unconquerable valor

That energized my wise stealthy hellraiser hutzpah trusting my rabble
rouser resolve that unleashed my percipient ability and puissant
agility to appreciate the situation by appreciating the situation

I instantly quit being a twit and squealing like a pig caught under
a gate telling everybody about everything that went wrong ingrains
that story in my subconscious encoding and unconscious codes

That never stopped sucker punching me because I kept hearing the
scaredy cat wishy-washy chatter that created today's subconscious
brainwashing unconscious paradoxes and my bullying bellyaching

Kept repeating the same paltry fables that kept recreating that type of
events according to my egoistically programmed belief's viewpoints
opinions and biased interpretations as I now realize and concede

I'm the only person that can entrench the complainer complacencies
so I instantly discharged and queried the fraudulent fury into
extinction as my nunow verve buzzes my natural nerve optimizes

My wonderful world of clairvoyant inlightenmint that sweetens my
ardor décor ascends my straightforward eloquence animates pioneer
brilliance to rise and shine beams my state-of-the-art artistic agility

Painting my wonderful world of luxury optimizing my stellar spiritual
daredevilry to understand and admit my unknown challenges are my
spirit's way of clearing out all my old worn out subconscious scams

Of damn and unconscious wastelands of bland instantly thrilling my
visionary valves of vibrant adventurous lore vigorously enterprising
altruistic love unleashing my awesome triumphs as I instantly

Fathom and admire my fun of the sun splendor as I soar over my current way of life to roar of royal omnific animated reveries esprit's my sprees of spiritual prescience intimately reveals imaginative

Treasures unleashed my nuwaves brave raving resolve that promptly discharged and disintegrated my braggarts BS so I trust my entrepreneurial skills that thrilled my wander's will to admire

My immaculate utopias of leisure within me that prompted my moviemaker imagination to unleash my Rembrandt brilliance that sketched and painted my murals of infinite panorama profusions

As I witness and smell the aromatic sea air tasting the mountain breezes hearing the mystique of desert as I set in my rocking chair of amazing riches as my sunny spirit beams my classy selfworth now and

Forever more I adore my liberation to deliberately enjoy my serendipitous bliss that streams thru all phases of my amazing life as I wholeheartedly embrace my ambling gamblers winners' delights

I Enterprized the Negativity

I electrified my souls' spectacular optimist's utopian lore stimulated my spiritual maturity and stouthearted spunk to ask... How has negativity and pessimism controlled the world since the beginning of time?

That rousted out my rebellious resolve to understand and esteem every life event is mirrors a tootsie pop because that chewy chocolate center mirrors my nuwaves of wisdom inspiration and inventive gifts

That hide in the center energizes mouthwatering flavors of stunning success as the hard candy coating is the shell of hell on the outside of a challenge chaos or untimed unsavory events so I now realize and

Admire I crack the shell of hell of the indecisive pessimism as I drink my nectars of nirvana extravagance celebrating today's awesome regal splendor as I stroll thru my day to day life in a healthy wealthy way

As I unbridled the negativity I let fly my Nowbirthed Enterprising Gumption Aggrandized Trendsetter Ingenious Visionary Intuition Tantalized yazzadazzled my vim venturer's daredevilry liberated

Me from me as I initiated nowborn confidence to understand and esteem I embedded stuff in my chronicled scenery that I'm oblivious to the way the programming interacts with my daily life so now

I cowboyed up and rousted out my rabble-rousing carousing investigative grit to uncover and eject my hidden blocks and worrywart torment to experience my inlightened festivities to wildly celebrate

My life my way instantly opened my hellraiser heart and cleared my sassy soul to voyage into my chronicled landscape with warrior verve to expand energize and enterprise my self-imbedded negativity

Into numinous electrified waves of space-age imagination wisdom
inspiration intuition innovative wit that let fly my trailblazer talent
as I say thank you and good bye to all my pessimistic paucity in

An emancipated loving way as I awakened to masterfully understand
and esteem today's negativity was a shrewd warrior that kept me safe
at certain time of my life as I now realize and value everything

That occurs within any life event is unique to that life event then it
converts into many things understanding wisdom new entrepreneurial
skills hidden blocks unrealized barriers and worrywart fears

That I'm clueless to the way it was implanted in the chronicled
countryside then becomes encoded images and memories in my
subconscious programming and unconscious representations

As I now understand and concede my feelings emotions memories and
everything I embedded are either innovative agonizing or unexciting
encoded messages so that opens my astute audacity to fathom and

Esteem the emotions feelings opinions viewpoints and memories are
activated by an outside activity involuntarily wakes up the feelings
emotions viewpoints opinions and memories that mirror that event

Then instantly instigates the utmost powerful representations and
programs that pertain to that event or events immediately trigger the
way I respond or react to that event as I now fathom and admire

My innovative acuity responds of fond with an onward and upward
articulated insight in a bold bright wonderful way as I swiftly
dethroned and unwound the agonizing reactions created

My disorderly retorts that spewed through me and out me to the world
passed out of me long ago as I instantly dismissed and exonerated me
myself and I from the involuntarily imposed limitations and unknown

Unsavory representations that snuck into my unconscious mind
is incognizant and lacks awareness and the capacity for sensory
perception subconscious mind is the part of my mind that deals with

Feelings and aware how feelings are imbedded and is activated now
as I avow with wow as I elegantly esteem my yesterday's negative
sarcasm is today's unpolished ingenious insight let fly trailblazing

Bravura elegantly energizes unconstructive negativity into nowborn
enterprising gumption animating trailbreaker artistic visionary
ingenuity titillates yazzadazzling daredevilry danced my neat feats

Of clairvoyant foresight escalating trailbreaker chutzpah that
disconnected and disintegrated the vile denial cynical crybaby criticism
and unraveled the groveling pessimists' prattle that rattled away

As I rattled my hocks of my head honcho optimism canonized kevalin
savvy that deliberately opened my eagle eyes and cleared my elephant
ears emblazoned my spirited acumen that clarified and eradicated

My obsolete neurotic nullifying negativity with illuminated
imagination wisdom inspiration intuition peerless prescience and
forthright fortitude unleashed my leadership valor and investigator

Skills so I confidently drilled down to the core to soar to boldly blast
my defunct pessimism out of date cynicism my hidden harassing
doom and gloom to smithereens sheens my backbone chi boomed

My optimist's oomph lightning bolts my zooming blooming state-
of-the-art brainpower excited my artistic brainprowess that lionized
omniscient omnific magic invigorating numinous grandeur purposely

Lit up my thoroughfares of financial freedom daring me to masterfully
to grasp and value my crabby cynicism prickly feelings and itchy
emotions are/were self-ingrained through the self-taught opinion's

ROBERT A. WILSON

Thinking and interpretations from my life experiences that are now
the behaviors opinions habits beliefs viewpoints thinking knowing
and memories that control my daily life as I now concede everything

I think and know comes from outside sources created my memories
either optimistic pessimistic or nondescript opened my majestic
gumption that unhooked being snookered by the scaredy

Cat skepticism that only talked and thought about unsavory things
that happened or can happen created the delusional judgments
throughout the inner landscape then the fearful buffoon acted out

In doubt because I tried look and live according outside sources then I
was forever looking for something or somebody in the physical world
for my way of life as I was living a subdued poopy do of following

Society's modus operandi compromised my dreams to follow people
that were talkers because people follow people that talk about what
they are going to do yet did zilch and shy away and stay away from

People that walk their talk and exhibit accomplished outcomes that
awakened to understand and admit people follow what other people
tell them makes people easier to control and they will follow anyone

That sounds good to them that stalemates people to stay stuck
in ancestral moldy old thinking knowing and memories because
trendsetter innovators that color outside the lines of the powers

To be are ridiculed by society's pecking order the media and by
politically correct people yet troublemakers are willing to fissure
societal structured herdocracy turdocracy by trusting and utilizing

Imaginative innovative inspirations are spiritually matured with fashion
designer gifts to charismatically color my divine pristine tranquility on
the heavenly skies as paint my Garden of Eden on my earthly vistas

That hued my harmonious utopia elegant splendor on my moneyed up
horizons strikingly charmed my dreamer's dexterity glorifying intrinsic
brilliance energizing rapturous animated optimistic nirvana to feel

I AM now grounded in wisdom understanding and admiring the
electromotive force of the universe unlocked and let fly my leader lithe
that discharged my trolling pessimism gleamed my liberating laser

Beams of love that broke up the cynical blocks pulverized them
into dust that blew away in my typhoon of triumph as my artistic
quixotic savvy illuminates my brilliant luminary elegance dawns

My sunrise splendor to awaken my bright bold heart love lumens my
sovereign classy selfworth that shows people a better way to live as I
write my nowography of rad liberation as I now amazingly admire

My maturity optimized my billionaire acuity as I bask on beaches of
bountiful bliss that kissed my life of Riley in a bright beautiful way
as my heart love shines so bright the angels are wearing sunglasses

Mystical Mess

I now realize and admire my life is a mystical mess that I expanded out of instantly manifests my miraculous blessings that electrifies my majestic energized stupendous success because my mystical

Messes unlock and exhilarate my enterprising supernatural savvy that is circling over my head because my emotions behaviors habits fear's flight fight or freeze mechanisms are embedded in my unconscious

Mind that is my data base that stores my endless information and records of my life events as the unconscious mind is the deepest of all the minds that helped shape my current thinking knowing minds

Viewpoints beliefs and opinions that are just embedded in my unconscious and subconscious minds and contain the map that controls the good bad or indifferent thinking and thoughts that I use

To communicate throughout my day that originated from everywhere created my current way of life by grasping this I stepped out of my previous world and rocketed into my wild blue yonder that thunders

My unknowable wisdom lightning bolts my brilliant omnific lore titillates spectacular adventures entice my venturesome vitality to treasure my mystical magical and miraculous messes with tranquil

Pleasure lets fly my unique mystique enterprising my spiritual savoir-faire flair zings my zestful nunow nirvana unleashes my nowborn enterprising wisdom and clairvoyant inspirations celebrating my life

Of liberation turned on my light of life lionizes inspirational farseeing enthusiasm as I asked me. How do I step back into yesteryear's thinking and knowing then instantly overthink today's events?

ROBERT A. WILSON

As I smile and dial up my Life of Riley as I now nobly admire I am
awarded my escalating mystical messes that bountifully blessed me
with present moment gifts of copious abundance in a loving way

As I now realize and admire my challenges chaos and unsavory
events are out of everywhere dares dawning audacious resolve
magnifying my charismatic charm to dance with my hellacious

Health wonderful wealth and stunning success unleashes globetrotter
gumption and oracle omnificence steams heats my farseeing feats
of financial freedoms floats me into holiday ecstasy as I entrusted

My numinous mystique excites mystical chi unleashed my supernatural
talent that energizes me myself and I as I now fathom and esteem my
spirit spontaneity relishes and embellishes my unfamiliar events

That energize venturesome glitz exalts numen nerve today unleashing
my charmed spiritual supremacies and astute clairvoyance as I now
recognize and admire my desired gifted outcomes are beyond

My current busy overthinking mind binded in yesterday's pessimism
or today's cynicism passed way yesterday as I now realize the numinous
magician within me hears and witnesses my life experiences through

My sixth sense trusting my gut feelings because my soothsayer
emotions and seers' feelings sense my unique life expanding wisdom
within every situation unleashes inventor's inspiration that unlocked

My pathfinder talents waltz me through my mysterious confusions to
majestically embellish spiritual splendor because a mess in my outside
world throws my inner world into turmoil all went away today

As all my enterprising senses sees straight thru the radical riddles of
every circumdance uncovering my mystical blessings as my guiding
light of liberation inspired galvanizing hellraisers trendsetter

Tenacity clearing away all dismay as I now play on fields of pristine
peace and mammoth money flow as I glow of mystical magical
miraculous magnificence beaming my gratitude and appreciation

Gleams my nowborn nirvana as I dissolved overthinking my life
is a stressful mess to understand and admire my life is mystical
mess unleashing my emotions supernatural sapience feeling

My forthright effrontery essence ignites my innovative nowborn
genius to stop living to what I know and think through my ingrained
memories of unsavory events because I now admit and get

I internally listen to unsavory events through insightful eyes and
emancipating ears with my unbewildering brilliance staring right
into the heart of my magical confusion that charmingly blessed me

Myself and I with out of this world success to rise and shine awakening
my boundless campaigner's lore dawning effulgent rainbows intuitive
noesis gusto letting fly nowborn nous that spectacularly strolls out

Of my befuddled unabashed adventures unleashed my yazzasizzle
savvy that heats up my maestro moxie that unflustered and dismissed
my brouhaha to feel the ahhh of my awesome hellraiser hutzpah

To embellish my mystical blessings that magically expands spiritual
sassy tenacity telling my human mind that is full of langsyne BS
that took a long wander stroll into the Sonora desert in August

As my autonomous utopian gusto unsheathed sightseer spontaneity
titillates eternal mastery escalating my nouvelle vague vibrancy
yazzajazzes my rollicking debonair flair exhilarated my gigantic

Jubilees of free celebrations unrestrained my meandering brilliance
optimizing my emotions stimulated sassy sovereign splendor because
my mess is internal yet I blame to external for my internal mess

As rainbow my external landscape I cleared out inner doubting mess
exalted my magical energizer bunny spunk uncluttered my funky gunk
setting sail on yacht of inquisitive wizardry untethered my sassy

Spunk to question everything that unclenches my beliefs opinions
and viewpoints to unlock my numinous paradises because every
challenge I embrace is/was to fissure my past or previous world
experiences that are memories up till 1 second ago as I now witness

My exquisite enchanted marvels arrive in my life now and forever
because I listen my glistening invisible mystical imagination glorifies
my inaudible intuitive innovative wisdom as I now realize and admit

The invisible inaudible are my frequencies of nowborn insight ignite
my light of intrigue initiating nunow treasures revealing innovative
gumption unleashing enterprising mystique that opens wherewithal

Bravura opening revolutionary nirvana because I experience my
unfathomable phenomenon's that are disguised as unsavory events
lets fly my inquisitive questioner to query's the furry of scurrying

My chaos and challenges into wisdom and inspiration that expands
me out of something from yesterday expanding me of my nowborn
glory as my spirit unravels mysterious messes that blesses me with

Majestic expansionism stimulating sovereign divine acumen to witness
and hear the mystical maverick wisdom inside the situation so I
stopped staying stuck on the surface of any situation to instantly

Awaken intuitive heart hutzpah and innovative soul savvy to let fly my
nowborn talents that rise from the confusion as I now embellish and
relish my life as royal blessings miraculously energizes stouthearted

Dignity steam heats my gladiator verve unsheathes my sword of
silent sapience to swiftly cut through the self embedded controlling
sabotage opening the way for my sail across the heavenly skies feeling

My spry wise debonair flair lit up the world with nirvana wisdom
inlightened inspiration and leadership talent as I dance with my
mystical magical miraculous selfworth that I opened my heart

Love unleashes my soul's splendor of utopian lore to realize and
admire life is an endless mysterious question for me facilitate and
participate of optimizing futuristic foresight ignites my light of life

To forever shine my divine felicity feeling loved and loving from within
me treasures my mystical messes with phenomenal pleasure now and
forever more my tropical utopia float's me onto my ultra-prodigious

Paradises as I received unlimited lavish abundances and gigantic
never-ending cash flow as I say Thank You to me myself and I all
people and the universe as I glide enjoying my red-carpet ride

That electrifies my traveler thrillpower energizes my hellraisers
liberated heart now and forever more I feel my wisdom breathes
bold rebellious fun of the sun spectaculars for me to enjoy

Subconscious Celebrations

I stopped using or saying the word mind to energize my conscious
festivities subconscious celebrations and unconscious vistas of vibrant
images scintillating treasured ardor scenarios of sunlit glitz

That awakened me to my astounding magnifying powers of inspiration
wisdom and celebrations that canonizes perpetual funloving festivities
energizes revered revelations adventurously trendsetting imaginative

Omnificence magnificently electrified my farseeing felicity that lit the
fires of my venturesome desires ignited my gut gumption galvanized
utopian moxie powered up my trailblazer intuition optimizing

Numen (divine power or spirit) acuity that rouse from deep within me
that let fly my daredevil dexterity dawning nunow esprit that steam
heats my hellraisers vigor aggrandizing torchbearer temerity jetted

My breathtaking brilliance that masterfully matured my intrinsic
innovative wit of willing intrepid trailbreaker intuition brought
to fruition my endless lavish financial freedom as I ask

How have I blocked myself thru my subconscious programmed limiting
beliefs that slyly controls my life today? As I now fathom and concede
my self-limiting programming stopped me from living my life leisure

As I ask... How did I teach myself societies selfish ways that
unconsciously programmed me to think there is never enough
abundance for me? As I discovered and uncovered I programmed

Myself to follow the lackluster seedy greedy needy and wanting
ways of societies recipes of delusion that I now grasp and admit I
naively entrenched in my chronicled minds that instantly opened

My liberating ardor to instantly quit repeating and trying to rewire
my old worn out structures to rebelliously dethrone and dissolve
my arrogant chronicled representations feeling sassy and classy

I instantly let fly my chronicled celebrations that illuminated my
shrewd enterprising lore energizing brilliant revolutionary acumen
tantalizing ingenious omnific gusto incited my sovereign poise

That clairvoyantly purified my farseeing optimists' luminosity
kinetically lionizing omniscient resplendence exhilarates my innermost
mystique to rise up and sheen my celestial pageantry daylight's

My dreamers' daredevilry decrees my frontiersman liberty to flow
through my venturer's veins of visionary effulgence as I recklessly
rousted out my rebellious spirit to realize my wise esteems

My core values are spine tingling resolve that dismisses and quiets
the boisterous bullies that try to ridicule me for me being defiantly
different and willing to color outside the lines of their fears endears

Me to my enterprising nerve dauntlessly enlivens awe-inspiring rabble-
rousing spunk that awaken my visionary venturer's lore to understand
and esteem to expand I stop rewiring anything to instill the thrills

Of nunow wow circuitry energizing my internal gumption harkens
trailblazer tenacity to rise and shine as I instantly expand to escalate
my life events with gratitude and enterprising vigor energizing

My numinous audacity masterfully esteeming I AM a beaming bold
light of love living optimistic vibrant elegance to masterfully admire my
forthright fortitude to understand and admire my nowfound fervency

I dislike my external life because I dislike my inner self and loathe
of disgust so to liberate me for me I went to a quiet place then wrote
all the info that was exposed to me from my chronicled wastelands

On paper then instantly rattled the hocks of all the puny pity me
prattle on to paper as got up out of the chair of dare and began
shredding the paper into little pieces to frankly discharge

The rat a tat crap as I walked by the waste basket with a sovereign
smile I threw my shredded worry into the waste basket giving it all
to the universe of liberation as now feel my chronicled splendor is

Sincerely free to I instantly hearkened cosmic magician that waved
her/his magic wand of charismatic charm instantly energized my
dreamer's audacity to trust my regal abilities that instantly spurred

My straightforward pluck to trust my moneymaker moxie dissolving
and disengaging my institutionalized viewpoints to instantly quit trying
to look and act tuff physically was me being a pretentious societized

Jellyfish because I was internally besieged by self-ingrained snooty
smug representations being stuffed with burping bratty snobbishness
trying to bluff my way through while being a blundering bully

Sulking and bulking walking around with a frown as I felt lost
tossed and bossed my unconscious effigies afraid of controversy
and adversity because adversity and controversy were beyond

My current knowing thinking and chronicled training that created my
worrywart gossip within me paralyzing my thinking knowing memory
minds that binded me in previous world or my past by admitting and

Grasping I did it I pulled lid liberating inborn chi that flew me into my
wild blue brilliance that instantly unbound my bold listeners dexterity
and astute communicative honesty letting fly my vibrant versatility

To listen effusively hearing my inaudible inspirations magnifies
my moviemaker magic energizing my maverick mystique of unique
accelerated me through my cheeky dexterity courageously let soar

My blunt stamina to listen and communicate my innovative
ideas invigorated my daredevil endeavoring acuity disconnected
and liquidated my tormenting twit and internally playing

The couch of grouch disrespecting myself and distrusting my core
strengths directly flew away because I woke to this crisp prodding
prudence my powerhouse of adventurous acumen that turned on

My brainpower that turned on my brainprowess to wow me out of the
fallacies of rewiring transforming or trying to change anything because
rewiring transforming and change are installed in the old fabric thru

My selftaught torment that controls my thinking knowing living from
memory unconscious codes of old that scrambles me back into the
same old ways of dismay because I stayed inside my thinking mind

With same old soceitized brainwashing rewiring is a retrofit with the
same structure with everything the same mundane mockery of me
myself and I as my new circuitry turns on my pacesetter resolve

Nobly stimulates omnipotent nerve to stroll of inspiration wisdom
and celebration as I let go the programming of change heal create
transformation forgiveness change and rewiring anything

I instantly zing and sang my songs of splendor optimizing nunow
gumption shining my hellraiser hearts energy realizing and admiring
to expand through life I energize imaginative inspiration enterprising

My innovative wisdom and subliminally celebrate my life experiences
with valiant voguish vibrancy that opens my eyes to understand life
was never ever to be controlled by yesterday's anything as I clear

My soothsayer savvies my soul senses my outlandish utopia loving life
because I stopped telling and thinking everything was going to occur
without a hitch and life was bland because of my self-taught torment

My subconscious representations thinking was perfect and everything was going to go perfect then when events went or awry in my antiquated programming made me think my life was hard creating

My self-induced thinking my life is a struggle which was my selfish way of being a greenhorn falling prey to my self-induced excuses that excused me from my dreams and life of leisure because I thought

I had to work and save instead of innovate and invest in myself to expand internally to be of intentionally chosen received wealth health and lavish abundances of all types a I awakened my subliminal

Celebrations I energized my inventor's gumption to hear the seers of the universe unlock my core inspiration spirit wisdom and cosmic celebrations as I now adhere trusting my new circuitry that freed

Me to let's fly first class with classy sassy smile of stouthearted sovereignty that to love my life thru my subliminal glorious gusto now and forever more I soar of spiritual and sovereign serene leisure

Supernatural

I now realize and esteem my supernatural gifts soar me above and
beyond my current thinking knowing and memorized way of life
as I now fathom and admire my supernatural elegance dances

My supra utopian pizzazz exhilarates revolutionary numinous
acumen trendsetting ubiquitous rapturous audacious lore lionizes
omnific revelations that catapults me into my universe's vista

Of visionary imagination stimulating trailblazer audacity opens my
spiritual maturity for me to fathom and esteem my space age forte's
glide me through the ultrasonic frequencies of the universe for me

To fly up to my galaxy of milk and honey as I land on my cosmic
runways of robust riches I tranquilly taxi to my penthouse of serene
leisure that instantly ignites my light of unexampled leadership skills

That thrill my rabble-rousing adventurous spontaneity optimizing
nomadic intuition celebrating and experiencing my day to day heydays
by trusting my supernatural ingenuity energizes my artistic flair

Dares me to trust my fashion designer flair that listens to the winds
of wisdom with my clairvoyant eyes wide open to hear my harmonic
enterprising acuity that revolutionizes omnific ultrabright trailblazer

Brilliance as I purposely received from everywhere that clarifies my
beautiful life of rapturous recreation coolvacious vacationers delights
and whatever else I desire to experience in a wealthy wonderful way

As my celebrations of liberation clear my sapient shrewd eyes to
witness the inaudible ideas floated to me from my cosmic magician
that waves her/his magic wand saying abracadabra instantly

My lush endless financial freedom and pristine peace are purposefully delivered to me in a natural bountiful way as I now masterfully admire the cosmic ceremonious waterspouts sprinkle warm colorful splendor

Of love health wealth and plush endless cash flow that is calmly supplied and awarded to me from my cosmic rivers of liquefied gold bullion that fills the universes endless whirlpools of minted treasures

That quickly appeared in my life because I showcased my grit get and go to rise up and glisten my divine charisma that magnetized the galaxies breezes of amazing bounty that I purposely manifested and

Delivered to my Garden of Eden festivals that energized my supra spontaneous charm that entices my inborn cosmic artiste to outline sketch paint and color the invisible inaudible and unexampled

Universe with my unique mystique mastery innovates my romantic paradises to be vividly visible to my sightseer eyes as I am wise with innerprising imagination and intuitive wizardry to appreciate and

Esteem I AM stylishly supernatural moven and grooven through life with a suave sense of humor to understand and admire me myself and I canonized my shrewd communication skills to amble through

My innermost uncharted charismatic celebrations that excite my day to day life opens me myself and I to my unrivaled aura of splendorous sapience that unlocks my celestial clarity lets fly my supernatural

Supremacy as I now feel my crisp clear idealist's acuity listens and witnesses the little things throughout my daily scampers that zing nowborn wisdom and innovation to energize big opulent outcomes

As my supernatural selfworth lets fly my spirit's ubiquitous insightful effulgence revolutionizes numen audacity trailblazing unexampled rapturous adventures loving life exuding a clever clairvoyance

Brightens my dreams imaginative wizardry intuitive charm unleashing
my state-of-the-art agility that unsheathed my thaumaturgy talents
to rise me above my current way living to shine my divine wininity

Of my supernatural willpower invigorates my nunow ingenious
nous instigating trendsetter yazzaspunk electrifies my sightseer's
communication with the invisible universe and physical world

As I now understand supernatural nous unsheathes my spry risk
takers vitality nobly optimizes unknowable savoir-faire gusto
galvanizes my classy sovereign me myself and I to my seer's

Fresh foresight I grasp the gleaming esteems energy of mystical
magical miraculous supernatural verve animated my yazzasnazzy
spirit electrified my spine-tingling prowess invigorating rebellious

Ingenious clarity appreciating loving my adventurous gumption
intimately celebrating amazing luxurious magnificence intuiting
revolutionary acumen canonizing utopian lore optimizing ubiquitous

Splendor gleams my tour de force unrestrained my inquisitive
questioner that extracted innerprising epiphanies s my yazzadazzling
pathfinder realized and admitted I shut down in a frown

By listening and following societies delusional despair that magical
events are make believe which was my self-inflicted thievery of
my dreams opened my supernatural eyes to masterfully admire

The mystical magical and miraculous are my marvelous unexampled
unexplained and unknown celebrations that occur throughout my
day to day extravaganzas energized my wraithlike cosmos fortified

My invisible intuition unleashed my inventor's blessings as I let fly
my ultra-bright foresight is beyond my book learning ancestor's
way of thinking and human limitations having to know before

I do or did anything stuck in scaredy cat anxiety that kept me thinking in timid torment until now as I disintegrated and dissolved my innermost turmoil unleashed my stouthearted trust of

My miraculous thaumaturgy that unfettered my mystical splendor that electrified my spectacular lore to feel the pristine perspicacity steam heat my hearts enterprisers animated revelations dignified

My spiritual maturity magically actuating triumphant trendsetter resolve intimately unlocks my puissant hellraisers audacious numinous thaumaturge to trust my feelings and emotions intertwining

My sixth sense the excite my brainpower the colors my brainprowess with incredible image of my moneyed up accomplished outcomes because my supernatural sensory acuity feels the outcome before

It occurs as optimizing clever canny undetailed revelations scintillating my emotions fortified my effrontery inlightenmint that sweetens my inner healthy wealthy inspirations wisdom and ritzy glitzy galas

Appreciating my ultimate upshots with glowing gusto gratitude as I now realize and admire my supernatural serendipitous bliss is inborn intuitive omniscient revolutionary nirvana because I now realize and

Admire I forever been awake and enlightened I AM now opening my feelings emotions inspirations wisdom and unalloyed talents to hear see touch taste and smell the invisible universe trusting...

My extrasensory instincts that instigates nirvana sapience titillating immaculate numen celebrations treasuring yipety serendipity admiring and embellish my streak of lucky pluck that unleashes luxurious

Earthly ecstasy celebrating kevalin serenity because I now understand and admire my supernatural acuity is alive letting my megaspirit energize my defeaters daredevilry cut-loose my numen nous excited...

My ultramundane enterprising acumen revving up torchbearer
hellraiser quixotic utopia aggrandizing kinetic ingenuity naturally
galvanizing my sunrise insights of ultra-liberating lore

That energized my clairvoyant curiosity that clears the way for
me to mature ESP showing me ty extraordinary savvy prescience
as prescience is pristine foresight to witness my life events on

My vertical time line feeling and witnessing my vibrant visionary valor
enticed my ingenious oracle optimizes my supernatural visions show
me my copious cornucopia upshots of my panorama leisure opens

My toddlers' eyes of idyllic innocence now and forever more I value
and esteem my omnific phenomenal blessings copious celebrations
with everlasting gratitude with classy sovereign appreciation and

A heartfelt hank You I straightforwardly express to the world
and all people as my supernatural abilities and agility energize
the universe and all people of a better way to experience life

Invest N Me Myself and I to Fly

I AM my intimate clever investor that initiates nirvana visionary
entrepreneurial savoir-faire flair within me titivates optimal
revolutionary decrees of investor ingenuity that opened my eyes

Of wise to my inborn omnific opulence that deposits my endless
streams of love lavish abundances and cashflow as I now fathom and
esteem I mature internally personally and spiritually to energize

My lush bounteous profusions that enterprises my plush infinite
cashflow as I cherish my life thru my streaming glitzy ritzy gusto
basking on my North Shores of Hawaii heydays as I directly awaken

My shareholder acuity to boldly and brilliantly invest N me myself
and I's intrinsic spectaculars coloring my subliminal scenarios with
holidaymaker wisdom panorama inspiration and globetrotter

Innovative gifts galvanize imaginative felicity titivates spiritual
maturity for me to trust my financier's wisdom feeling self-assured
throughout my daily strolls of stunning success impeccable

Health and ever flowing fiscal autonomy relishes and embellishes my
Shangri La sovereignty as I celebrate my life of pristine serenity as I
now fly freely decrees I intentionally savor my fabulous yazzyjazzy

Lifestyle as I glow of gratitude lionizing optimist's charm frees me to
appreciate and trust my spine-tingling valor to expand beyond my
knowing thinking mind unwinds my utopian nomadic clever visions

N livens stylish integrity and spirited morality to realize and
esteem I AM marvelously shrewd deliberately admiring I AM
elaborately flourishing with a humorous wit to internally witness

My sumptuous success on my physical plane of fame as I feel
awesome magnificent elegance exhilarates my investigator's grit to
uncover discover and unleash my invest N me vigor mystically

Animates my entrepreneurial skills enterprising my minted proficient
finales as I Am thee financier with a dazzling imaginative nous
augmented my valiant investors courage invigorated colossal

Regal treasures as I thrust my intrinsic innovative savvy into my
game of life unsheathed my vibrant gallantry validates my gamers
gumption that strolled me onto my stage of award-winning

Triumphs realizing and honouring my world-shattering achievements
as my inner billionaire flair magnetizes my innermost investor
lore energized my loyal trust of abilities highlights my investors

Inlightenmint that sweetens self-respect for my sagacity brilliance
and pioneering legacies that instantly dissolved and terminated my
stubborn hardheaded selfishness briskly awakened my heart and

Soul to beautify my selfworth to experience my bounteous luxury as
I now realize I invest in my intimate nunow venturer's vitality thrilled
my spiritual tour de force that illuminated my inner minted treasures

With keen kinetic gusto zooms my kevalin elucidation that ripened
my celebrating optimism invigorating nunow splendor that effortlessly
flow through my veins of fame as I flowingly feel my dazzling royal

Spontaneity salsa me through life as I now fathom and admire my
spicy inborn investors acuity awakened and aggrandized my spiritual
perspicacity enterprises endeavoring flights of fancy prescience freed

My animated reveries invigorating panorama gratitude as I now
appreciate and declare I encompass grit get and go that galvanized
omnipotent clairvoyance to straightforwardly invest in me

Myself and I to fly innerprisingly shrewd to majestically expand my inner wisdom magically energize spectacular thrillpower enterprising my pathfinder chi fabulously esteemed my inborn ingenuity hotly

Electrified my stellar pacesetter poise to understand and admire I embody unique talent to invest within me and expand the world wisdom inspiration and innovation honouring Iwon externally

As I enchantingly colored my lustrous celebrations through my inner scenery sheens my charismatic charming felicity to expand my fashion designer brilliance energizes and enterprise my life as I AM

Thee stockholder on my moneyed up accomplished outcomes and the recipient my profuse boundless financial blessings as I bask on my beaches of relaxation and mountains of milk and honey sitting

On my pinnacle of peace as my stupendous victor's verve enlivened today's enterprising nibbana that instinctively opened my unexampled magnificence enlivened my visionary vim that unsheathed

My unexplainable wisdom ultradazzling inspirations and megastar talents that I never knew or had a clue I encompassed because I know and think on the surface of my brain as my wisdom is my profound

Daring lore that floats up to awaken my intuitive curiosity that excited inquisitors' artistry that colored my subliminal scenery with my affluent realizations from my intrinsic investments that I enjoy now

As I now grasp I ask forward-looking open-ended questions that query my current way living calling out my fears exposing my scaredy cat bratiness illuminating my inner landscape with gleaming

Esteemed gallantry that sheens my sassy hellraiser entrepreneurial enthusiastic numen sapience that dances my dreams esteemed elegance through my conscious setting with venturesome vigor and

Ambling ardor cultivated out my doubters' weeds of needy greediness
because I tenaciously trusted my sovereign acumen autonomous
agility and trailblazer audacity magnetized the universe with

My sanguine wisdom gusto inspiration and supernatural talent they
encompassed that energized their confidence and courage to hear the
ascending acumen traveler's mettle and spirit talents that cleared

My trails of triumph to treasure my abundant accomplished outcomes
with poetic pleasure as I AM skywriting my poems of poetic peace and
plush prosperity on cosmic skies of celebrations to realize and value

Embracing and investing in my inner nunow vibrancy expanding savvy
trailblazer imagination naturally tantalizing my innerprising prowess
energizing my enterprising intuition hearing my prospering inaudible

Acumen electrifying my innovative wit to shit and get up my trails of
lavish endless abundances I received with gratitude and appreciation
for my abilities all people and universe's endless surpluses of scenic

Copious cornucopia of all styles as I now understand and admire my
investor maturity chosen to intentionally woke up my confidence
courage and selfworth to celebrate my life of lush plush delight

Lit up my autonomous audacity instantly deleted my dark
controlling recordings of yesterday to sing hit songs of hellraisers
gusto that galvanizes ultrabold savvy trendsetter optimism

Of my investor savvy magically energized my artistic spiritual
magnificence today opening my investors intuition to invest N me
myself and I swiftly enlivened my numen vigor that escalated

My self-trailboss mystique yazzajazzes stouthearted eminence
lionizing fervency aggrandized nervy daring I AM liberated investor
that understands me myself and I stopped telling the stories

About anything that happened in my life opened my nowography
eloquence expressing my inspired fiery foresight to appreciatively
admit and admire every event I experienced in my life are uniquely

Timed life expanding events that opened the way for me to be aware
of dare to experience my nunow wow as I witness the earths airwaves
feeling the warm glowing grandeur that fantastically fashions styles

Colors and paints my dreams on every horizon I observe in my day
to day life so I witness hear smell taste touch trusting my magnetism
to receive my moneyed up miracles instantly as I now understand

My imagination lumens my dreams energize my sunrays of praise
exhibits my divine fashion designs instantly excited my mystical
designer excites my Picasso prowess my paints a colorful blossoming

Vrooming portrait of my desire life that I experience now and forever
more soaring of spiritual supremacy feeling my investor maturity
relishing and embellishing I am grounded of gratitude and appreciation

Dared Me

I dared me to experience my life thru my rabble-rousing carousing
eyes that spurred my globetrotter grit get and go galvanized
my omniscient head honcho hutzpah to realize and admire

My firebrand insight unleashed my wave maker courage to
discharge and disconnect all the antiqued beliefs viewpoints and
opinions that thrusted my rebellious rocketeer into action

That blasted me off my couch of grouch and ascended me to glide
over and beyond my current way of life with a double dare flair that
strolled me thru my day to day life with my core warrior will thrilling

My troublemaker troubadour to write and sing songs with luminous
liberated lyrics as I straightforwardly dared me to only sing speak and
write about my dreams and accomplished outcomes experiencing

My beautiful bountiful paradises of peaceful prosperity and prosperous
peace as I instantly rolled the dice that enticed my gamblers foresight
ignited my hellraisers decrees I freed me from me and immediately

Emancipated my innerprising ingenuity that surprised me with
ultrautopian charismatic wizardry that initiated my astute empire-
building audacity that promptly electrified my moneymaker

Spectaculars triggered my spirited pathfinder parties canonizing
torchbearer acuity decrees my maestro brio creeds rev up my
exhilarated my spirit's pageantry that outright dared me to soar with

The eagle's salsa with grizzly bears and swim with the Orca's as I
now apprehend and admire my day to day life is a rapturous glamour
that majestically paints my heaven on earth horizons with

My wild blue yonder with ultrabright neon nirvana rainbow's my
multicolored animated grandeur invigorated zestful optimistic zeal that
dared me to show all the people and the world my sassy classy sex

Appeal as I witnessed firsthand I encompassed that poise to expand
out of yesterday to expand of my nunow wow that energized my walk
of wisdom festivities enterprized my wise optimists will that minted

My thrills and frills that ignited my dazzling fun of the sun splendor
excited my vacationer's vitality relishing my holiday galas feeling alive
and energized rebelliously yelled hell yes I ride and glide trusting

My rancher's upfront agility adoring my hellacious rich legacies to
sleep under the stars feeling fresh like the air after a spring rain as I
experienced my fantastic fame fabulous fortunes and elatedly value

My daring debonair flair to appreciate my intrinsic spunk that dared
me to daylight my lionhearted audacity that triumphantly embellished
my swashbuckler spontaneity to realize and admire my life dared me

To stand up with my head high shoulders back knees straight trusting
the invisible forces of universe to reward me for my will to appreciate
and expand through the unfamiliar fiestas feeling my victor's gusto

As I hastily quit and dethroned my accepting yesterday's way of life
and living down the societies self-serving arrogance allowing outside
sources to have power over me as I decree I AM free glistens my rad

Selfworth that energized my farseeing felicity instigates shrewd
insight that canonized yazzasnappy spunk esteems my gleaming
gumptions that Dared Me to tango to the beat of my idealist's fortes

That dauntlessly animated my royal euphoria that mystically
energized my awe-inspiring brilliance that unraveled my unexampled
numen lore that enriched my majestic ecstasy feeling my kevalin

Vitality to feel honourably rebellious exhilarating my free will to embrace all my sassy dares as I understand and admire my unsettling events are my uncharted gifts that generate imaginative foresight

Trendsetting stunning bliss to be my way of life as I instantly disintegrated and quit flopping around like a fish out of water when an uncomfortable event popped up because I rapidly electrified

My venturesome abilities and explorer's agility branded my confident and courage to understand and admit it is easier to stay inside societies primitive habits with representations to be afraid

Of everything with a sky is falling stuck in their craw of bah humbug spewing their cackling crap about all the ways everything going awry bellyaching about anything that was beyond their thinking

That are ingrained beliefs habits and patterns stopped here and now as unhooked my wanting to look good in other people eyes instantly I stopped criticizing and despising myself internally externally and

Eternally debunked putting a on charade I smarter than somebody else was my paralyzing blather that rattled yesterday's pity me prattle within me crossed river forever to extinction as I realize and admire

My outlaw optimism opens unorthodox pacesetter lore animated my wily wisdom to miraculously maneuver through situations with sassy heart hutzpah unclogged my valiant trailblazer intuition innovating

Nowborn guru brilliance lighting up animated zeal enthuses rabble rousing sightseer savvy to rise from my romanticists rapturous revelations dance's my dared me moxie through my venture's veins

Of vibrant enthusiastic inventor's nous stimulating my innate leadership majestically extolling my elegance that romances my swashbuckler pizzazz that powers up my intramural zest zeniths

My amazing jazzy zeal shines my feisty visionary sex appeal wheels
and deals my idealists energetic audacity lumens intrinsic nibbana
gallantry frees my grinning galas energizes my celerity celebrations

That opened my romantics eyes expanded my entertainer's spunk
that buzzed my bold utopian fervor zings my zensational inner peace
to massage my extrinsic landscape with sovereign serenity sheens

My regal balmy peace that easily and effortlessly dawn my esteemed
enterprising splendid cutting-edge endeavoring extravaganzas
magically entertaining dazzling utopia feeling omniscient opulence

Flows through me as I celebrate my emancipated emotions liberated
feeling and subconscious celebrations powered up my light of life
splendidly sensing my nunow wow of wonderful optimistic will

That thrills my divine sovereignty to understand I dethroned all my
hidden funk flushing my hidden gunk down the stool as I AM now
my farseeing entertainer strolling effortlessly through life with beams

My numinous luminous inspirations excited my kevalin knight
influenced and powered up my illuminated flame of love magnifies
nunow revelries energizing my backbone bravura electrifying today's

Wonderful heydays to play on pastures of pure coherence and lush
opulence feeling my emotions sassy classy sovereignty flow through
veins of fame feeling my audacious majestic freedoms expanding

My listening enthusiast's spunk unleashing my innerprising life force
gushing my enterprising wizardry letting fly my entrepreneurial skills
that thrilled my risk taker tenacity that turned on my backbone

Brilliance energizing my spine-tingle bravery to boldly love life
openly canonized my kevalin energy to flow through life beaming
my optimists grin winning ways shine my victorious valor across

The cosmic skies as I beam eternal optimism through me to the
world showing people a better way to experience their life of Riley
as I witness and admire my wave after wave of optimum health

Wealth and my wonderful world of trendsetter tutors and mystical
metaphors that open the way for my spirit sovereignty to soar lionizes
my enlightened nirvana fame rococo's my yazzadare flair polishes

My brassy sassy self-worth waltzes me out of town to treasure my
holiday festivities that opened my heart eyes and cleared my souls'
ears to witness I dared me to mature superbly unsheathed

My sprees of divine autonomy that intentionally delivered me
my amazing life that I appreciate with gratitude as I dared me to
experience my magnificent expansionism of epic spiritual maturity

Illuminated my intimate paradises showing me my external galas
now and forever more I saunter on to my beautiful beaches of
bountiful healthy bliss as I relish my prosperous peaceful paradises

Detached Panache

I feel my detached panache unlatched my snazzy classy savvy
leadership skills that waltz me thru life with a rebellious utopian
mojo boldly appreciating all my life events that beautifully endear

Me to my spirit flair that exhibits my rare breed credence to celebrate
my ground-breaking entrepreneurial daredevilry energized my cutting-
edge innovative thrills that lovingly spills my princely blessings

Of my over-the-top cornucopias into my lap as I set on my front
porch of tranquility looking into the universe's tabula rasa canvas
of celebrations aggrandizing nirvana visions animates stupendous

Understanding that the universes vista is featureless blameless and
depersonalized until I interject my stylish innovations into the
universe's landscape that begins journey for me to expand energize

Enterprise and experience the events that broaden my trailbreaker
talents to facilitate and participate on my paths of moneyed up
accomplishment that opened my heart eyes souls' ears to witness

My sparkling blue skies authorizes me to look outward and through
my terra incognita scenarios awakens my map artiste that silhouettes
my Garden of Eden on my subliminal countryside by engaging

My hi-tech foresight unleashes my fashion designer insight that
initiates my visionary outlines imaginative representations that awaken
my visionary mappers that crafted my ingenious sketches for

My Picasso artistry to color and paint my mystical map of my dreams
and life of relaxing leisure on my pure clear canvas that displayed
my pristine scenery of my panorama paradises on my third eye

Movie screen and all phases my amazing life feeling my electrified
felicity and fervor enthusiasm that flows through me as I frankly feel
my elegant health extreme wealth illuminated love venturer's vitality

Nomadic nous and lavish endless money flow that I purposely
received with a smile of appreciation and a grin of gratitude that I love
and enjoy in a bold bright way today and every day in every way

As I play on pastures of green serene luxury now and forever more I
now realize and esteem my detached panache salsa's me through life
to experience hellraiser fun sensing poetic peace stream through...

Me expanding and electrifying my world of moviemaker magic that
abracadabra's my heavenly holidays adoring my ceaseless amusement
park excitement as I entrusted my detached panache that quickly

Emancipated dethroned and tossed my antiquated crabby crotchety
rat a tat crap that secretly controlled me from childhood till now
into the ocean of oblivion that fertilized my oceans of optimism

Seas of tranquility and magical mountains of unique mystique
ubiquitously powered on my traveler's imagination enterprising my
oracle omnificence illuminated my ultrabright grandeur as I see

My life and world through toddlers' eyes unbridled my pathfinder
heart and stellar soul that stimulated my optimist's utopian lore
to understand and admire the mysteries of me the riddles

Of my inborn selfworth confusion of my physical world and the silence
of my eternal cosmos awakened my ramblers resolve and gamblers
nerve to escalate the mystical magical miracles I uncovered and

Discovered in the caramel centers of my rollicking life expanding
riddles of my dream's mysteries of me confusion and silence as
I hastily laundered and cleared my animated clairvoyant

Acuity that hearken my calm classy sapience from the silent insight
of mystic Inlightemint the energized my supernatural imagination
wisdom inspiration and innovative gifts that arrived in my life for me

To elucidate and validate my intimate nowfound foresight treasuring
my daily celebrations esteems my enterprising emotions and visionary
feelings that wonderstruck my optimistic globetrotter gumption

That astonished my omnipotent torchbearer emboldens my state-of-
the-art omnificence exalts my visionary delights excited my genius
eloquence geysers my guru acumen thru the earth's airwaves

With a booming zooming frequency of fun recreation enjoying quiet
utopia elegance nobly celebrating admiring yes I am blessing boldly
loving every day serendipitous splendor initiating nunow glamour

That exhilarates my effrontery resolve shining my divine daredevilry
thru me energized my lucky frequencies to flow through the
worldly airwaves unlocking people's empire building bravery

As I now grasp and galvanize my intrinsic wise wherewithal fathoms
and esteem I encompass the gut gall to ride through my challenge's
chaos and tragedies with my lance of liberation discharging and

Disconnecting all the unfriendly feelings unfavorable emotions
pessimistic thoughts thinking and memories in a loving way extols
my keen warrior dignity aggrandizes my gala nibbana dawns

Spine-tingling sapience that instantly heralded my insight brilliance
ingenuity and spontaneous innovations from my vanguard visionary
vibrancy enlivened my divine designers' talents that charted and

Mapped my unknown inaudible unexampled and unexplained
countryside with spectacular scenarios of my Promise Land luxury
as I unsheathed my detached panache of my inventor's brainpower

That motorized my artistic brainprowess of my nunow wow robustly
rousted my omnipotent optimism of my nowborn visions and my
pioneering nous that unhoused and deloused my vanity that kept me

Stuck in my flack of lack as I quit being delusionally whacked about
unusual things in my life now and forever more I immediately expand
out of my minds because my minds bind me in my blemished

Feelings and emotions that kept me stuck in flight fight or freeze blight
that flow through my mouth to the world with anchored angry retorts
as I trained myself anger made me look tough was a lie yet selfish

Angry people are internally weak because anger steam heats self-
sabotage as I now admit and grasp anger is bluff of inbred scaredy
cat bratiness cleared myself delusional despair that unseated and

Ended my doubt with my ascending inlightened love illuminating
my hearts heavenly glow and soul's sunny pageantry instantly
unleashing my detached daredevilry of my supreme

Spiritual supremacy as I radiantly beam my debonair flair across
the earthly skies skywriting sovereign kinetic intuitive eloquence
stimulates my innate talents to gleam I AM sacredly sovereign

As I instantly awakened to my emancipated verve to vigorously
expand my rebellious elegance to dance thru glorious me as I
serenely salsa through my physical world waltzing with

My eternal splendor as I soar of ultimate puissance as I immediately
blasted my bitching and bellyaching to smithereens as I sheen
my hellraiser hearts harmonizing wizardry through

The universe shining my soul's autonomy optimizing utopia love
to flow and glow avowing my life is a divine decree of liberation
feeling my royal vim expand my dauntless omnipotence

Mystically illuminated my majestic miracles within me that naturally invigorated rabble-rousing vigor audaciously enlivened my wise animated poetic affluence relishing my easy street

Living thriving of detached panache waltzing with my fancy-free festivities feeling my emotions streaming my trailblazer artistic state-of-the-art treasures that initiated my exotic safaris

That escalated my innate movie maker moxie as I glide on cloud nine wining and dining on divine love now and forever more as I understand and admire my wisdom optimizes utopia treasures

Celebrating opulent majestic enjoymint feeling my sweet grandeur flow through my veins of vitality showing me my lavish luxurious leisure as I witness and admire my grit get and

Go manifested my fame and fortunes in a light bright gracious way As I say Thank You to the invisible cosmos to all people and the universe as I gleam of zestful gratitude and appreciation

Dissolving Perfection

I awakened to understand and concede I taught myself to think
that everything I wanted to do was going to go perfect and end
in perfection without a challenge just like I had it drew up in

My thinking mind and egotistical arrogance thinking there would
be zero glitches because it was my idea and everything will move
along perfectly because of my pompous conceit and know it

All ignorance because the definition of egotistical ignorance is the
know it all inexperienced thinking they know it all as I now realize
and admit when things go awry my spry cosmic magician interjects

My nowbirthed life expanding innovative ideas and a better way for
me to expand me out of the mystical messes that introduce me to my
empire designer acuity that unshackles me from me that expanded

Me out of yesterday into understanding today is the day I energize
my nunow wow illuminates my walk of wisdom celebrations whirls
my waltz of wondrous serendipitous brainpower that kissed me

With intuitive ingenuity thrilled my gladiator gumption that rocketed
my confidence courage and audacity to understand and admire my
imperfections shine my classy character as I grasp and admit

My imperfections were pointed out to me according to other people's
uncertainties because insecurities compare and categorize people
according to their recorded representations so I strolled away

In a dynamic way unleashed my maverick mettle saunters me out
into the world with trailboss willpower optimism revolutionizing life's
doughty daredevilry instantly and lovingly discharged and unhooked

My thinking everything I do was perfect and is done with perfection
that kept repeating the same inane thoughts every day as my inner
landscape was busy overthinking with murky fusspot chaos causing

My doubter debris to raise up and control me created the anxious
stressful thinking just waiting for the everything gone wrong song
to play because perfection creates yesterday today and today will

Be repeated tomorrow thru my biased thoughts of I'm perfect
other people and the world are messed up and its never me that
all went away as I hastily dismissed and debunked the know it

All ignorance and egotistical conceit that slyly governed my life
causing today to be same as all my yesterday's as I now liquidate
and surrendered my trying to be perfect and all my insults about

Perfection I admit was my immaturity massaging my ego and setting
me up for some unsavory events since perfection and perfect are fake
and bake trickeries of big-headed pride that induced my crabby

Self-centered couch potato prattle that rattled on and on about
everything with an underlying porous pout was my skeptical
delusions of my silent tormenting troll that harassed me internally

So I energized my gut moxie that dethroned and disconnected all of my
old worn out thinking and knowing dissolved the mincing memories
that I hide from the world that I'm afraid to admit I encompassed

As all my hidden haunts chained me to yesterday's pain so today I
broke the chains of pain animated my fame and fortune vigor that
thrilled my rebellious resolve that initiated my canny hero's brio

That yazzadazzled my puissant spirit spunk to understand and
embellish my instinctive sublime grit galvanized my day to day life as
my enterprising game of generating moneymaking miracles opened

The way for me to play on pastures of lush prosperity manifesting and attracting people that ask me life expanding questions as I tune out people that talk about how perfect they are as I brazenly liberated

Me myself and I to glide from their controlling categorizing ways to awesomely exhibit my charismatic charm to the world let fly my imperfections ascend my imaginative mystique that powers up

Ingenious rapturous foresight eulogizes clever trailmaker innovative omnific nirvana opens my core trust in my sovereign abilities that dethroned my perfection thinking that was old and worn out

Cloudy doubt barricaded zero new because my mind is busy talking and talking about what is going wrong in my life talking about what everybody else has doing wrong and the way I do cutting them

Down verbally because I thought I would do a better job was the pompous parrot mimicking me spewed the pooh in the stew about what I did yesterday emitting the sarcastic rat a tat crap

That continuously zapped my energy as I laid on the couch grousing about everything blaming everybody for my life situations never getting off my bench of stench yet my trying to be perfect was

The know it all inexperienced rookie that woke up spewing the shaming shams of I'm perfect as I swiftly blamed everything and everybody involved in the situation as the needless insidious insults

As my egotistical perfection placed me on pedestal of paralyzing prattle that rattled my raging cage of ridiculing rancor was the way I reacted to my daily events with juvenile resentment sinking into

Delusional despair because my anchored anger controlled my reactions so I dissolved my thinking I was perfect disintegrated my reactive retorts opened my listener troubadour to sing my lyrics

Of love polishing my opulent oratory wit to communicate events
energizing my lavish life of moneyed up bliss that brightened literary
luminous energy majestically innovating supernatural hutzpah

Electrifying serendipitous gusto as I now admit and dissolve I grew up
trying to be perfect putting undue pressure on myself then I would try
to act like zippo mattered yet it did to the emotional insecurities and

Embedded immaturities that were active inside me I with me being
afraid to let to trying to be perfect in my daily life to understanding
and admiring my life maturing hurdles I encounter thru my day

As I now cognize and relish my life is fascinating mysterious mess that
flows with magical mishaps and mystical mayhem that supernaturally
liberated me and discharged the humanoid annoyances of being

Worried about how I looked in other people's eyes were my
quiteyetice twiteyetice created my dysfunctional delusions created my
egotistical missile of mayhem always bumbling stumbling through

Events bitching and bellyaching about everything then scrambling to
cover up something that went awry so I would shied away in blame
feeling emotionally charged sabotaging shame avoiding my dreams

As I now realize and admit I AM innovatively imperfect in the
human world yet pure spiritual inspiration listening to my spirit savvy
energizing my celestial celebrations to admire my blemishes brightly

Beam luminous enterprising mystique innovating stouthearted
hutzpah enlivens stunning success as my wise that swiftly energizes
my ingenious ingenuity thrills my campaigners nerve that waltzes

Me down my trails of triumph brightly beaming my grin of Iwon
thru the universe sheens my inborn willpower opened my playful
wherewithal glory within me steam heats my esteem selfworth

To bask of my sun of the fun felicity relaxing in my sun thrilled
serendipitous bliss in the sweet caramel center copious cornucopia
tasting the sweet sumptuous milk chocolate celebrations of my life

Lighting up inspired fervent energy to realize and esteem my
blemishes and imperfections are my nowborn enlightenmint that
sweetens my artistic talents to paint my intrinsic canvases with hues

Of hellacious utopia as I paint my extrinsic universe with murals of
magnificent ubiquitous rich affluent luxurious splendor now and
forever more I love my imperfections and blemishes that brightens

My Garden of Eden ecstasy with exquisite miraculous intimacy sheens
hellraisers enterprising savvy to expand me through everything feeling
and expressing zestful gratitude and appreciative audacity trusting

My venturesome vigor feeling healthy wealthy wise and love
unconditionally and unselfishly expressing my heart love
to myself and the all people in a big bright bold way

I Cut Rat A Tat Crap

I cut the rat a tat crap to disengage and stop romancing my past
through drama and trauma that created the rhetoric of how chaotic my
life was making me sound like a superhero to my snobbish conceit

Yet my innermost representations were looking for sympathy wanting
people to feel sorry for me that made me grouch and nitpicker so I cut
the rat a tat crap discharged and disconnected the self embedded

Drama trauma and trying to make my life sound good through drama
like a soap opera that made me the star of my soap opera that fueled
my insecurities and immaturities make me think my childhood was

More challenging than others so people would feel sorry for me and
cut me some slack was the fake and bake quackery going on inside of
looking for help mind yet I was actually looking for somebody to do

Everything for me came to a screeching halt as I catapulted up and
out to understand I honourably listen for the wisdom to expand me
onto my roads of riches so I stopped trying to take the easy road

That created my rat a tat crap that controlled my life because the
drama was self-taught so I nobly cut the crap to rap to revolutionize
appreciate participate and facilitate my saunter onto my Shangri La

Paradises as I realize and admire zero occurs in my physical world
that can affect me intrinsically unless I'm allowing my outer world to
control me as I spurred my engendering spontaneous trailblazer grit

To ask How do I resist anything new beyond my current thinking
knowing and memories? As I taught myself to resist new to stay safe
inside what I know then being afraid of my artistic brilliance instead

I heard my egotistical wastelands of wanting needing material chattels
to think I was impressing somebody that depressed me internally
because I now dismissed and discontinued trying to impress others

That smothered me in greedy seedy sabotage I put myself through
because I was looking for approval from others all stopped the instant
I cut my crap to immediately of approve of me myself and I

To fly feeling lionhearted yazzapanache that optimistically electrified
my thrillpower to admire my inborn scenery manifested everything
I desire to experience my endless sumptuous divine abundances

As I woke this morning with my hellraisers hutzpah running wild
and lustfully willing to concede and dissolve I'm the resistance of
everything that kept me stuck in my survival mode existence that…

My poverty conscious map kept me imprisoned inside thru insecurity
immaturity and immobilizing paucity because my guilty indignity
programming kept rerunning everything I thought I did wrong

According to my societized upbringing that I feel prey to by
embedding what other people said that went along with I'm never
good enough corrupted thinking I did to myself put up my wall

Of stalling know it all ignorance and head up my ass egotistical
arrogance was my rat at tat crap criticizing rhetoric afflicting paucity
palaver spewing yesteryears jeers of sneering worrywart snapback

Rat at tat smart aleck answers of deception because I used deception
to cover up my innermost self-doubt and futility so I quickly
discharged and disconnected the innermost self-loathing and futility

That all passed away today as I awakened my rabble-rousing resolve
to evolve of enterprising visionary omnificence lionizing victor's
eminence to dance with my inaudible wizards' invisible innovators

Unexampled talents unexplainable inspiration and unseen utopian
lore foresure I awakened my venturer's soul and adventurous heart to
shine my light of love from open my heart that harmonizes eternal

Animated revelations tantalizing my thrilling shrewdness to fathom
and admire the stratosphere of splendor is my faucet of canny
imaginative reveries canonized my intuitive scenery sensationalized

My ceremonious epiphanies neon's my multicolored magnificent
ubiquitous luminesce treasures invigorating canonized optimism of
imaginative spiritual maturity that excited me that unchecked and

Let fly my campaigner's candor robustly trusting sassy tenacity to cut
loose my crap to crack my whip of wise hellraisers inventors poise that
modernized my intrinsic brainpower that energized my brainprowess

That wowed me to fathom partake and accelerate my supernatural
savvy that hearkens my spirit winds of expansionism that instantly
stimulates mystical ingenuity to awaken my troublemaker curiosity

To candidly unleash my rococo ingenious terra incognita sapience
invigorating trendsetter yazzasassy state-of-the-art skills that thrill
me and unsheathed forerunner troublemaker that friskily fissures...

My unconscious worrywart retorts that are embedded deep in my
thinking know memory mind subconscious programming and habits
in the way I communicate with others because I had a get revenge

Unknowingly ingrained in my innermost wastelands that stained my
brain with sabotaging snobbish impish wishy-washy turmoil and to say
unsavory things to or about others trying to hurt them while thinking

I was putting them in their place but in truth and honesty I was
putting me myself and I into wimpy timid torment snobbishly thinking
I was being a tough stand up person was a flat-out fallacy I told

Myself so I slashed that crassy prattle to expressing my heartfelt
good will to all authorized myself and the other participants to stroll
away today and every day in every way wiser articulate people

As I now understand and esteem I awakens my invisible oasis through
open ended questions instantly cleared the way for my inquisitive
wizardry to unlock my Promised Land of plush lazy boy setting...

Clarified my out of this world health wealth and thrillpower to waltz
of rapturous love dawning a new era of enterprising riches aggrandizing
my life of lavish leisure as I now under and esteem cut the crap

Opens my gut gall to stop hearing my habitual foolish fodder that is
my current way of life as I now admit and get I followed the school
books my circle of influence the school system and societies social

Odor of money and wealth rule was the loser's larceny of myself
taught herdocracy turdocracy because I kept stepping in mine and
other people rat at tat crap thinking I was going somewhere was a

Fib of never live my way of life strife as I now admit and express to
the world following other people and using books as an absolute
polluted my inner landscape because following and adoring myself...

To understand books written by others is they want me to know so
now I hearken and harvest their wisdom and innovative wit to inspire
my dreamer's acuity and venturer's validity to manifest my moneyed

Up accomplished outcomes dreams delight and my life of lavish
tranquil holiday harmonies foresure as I candidly awaken to cutting
my inner rat a tat crap as I now understand and admit my inner rat a

Tat crap was the hidden resistance to my heaven on earth experience
because as I now realize and value my heaven is my pristine inner
peace my pastures of serene peace awakens my receptivity

That adheres me to y invisible cosmos illuminates canny optimist
savvy magically optimizing splendor because my heaven is my
euphorically ecstasy I feel my spiritual sanctuary that opens

My esprit to feel spontaneous sovereignty flow through my veins of
vibrant ingenious imponderable nous sensualizing my wanders wise
invincibility to invigorate nowborn visionary intangible nirvana

Celebrations instigating brilliant imaginative lore titillating
yazzacuriosity to clear away my humanized debris frees my sprees of
supernatural prowess revs up spiritual spontaneity to admire the

Glistening sunrises of my unseen cosmos energizing my rumba
of lavish endless bountiful bliss that brilliantly lights up intrinsic
spontaneous splendor unleashing my adventurous ardor...

To soar of spontaneity opening amazing robust money flow for
me myself and I to enjoy now and forever more I feel my matured
eloquent lexes of energized inspirations expands me and all people

My World of Words

I unleashed my visionary vibrations that magnetically salsas with my
world of words that energize my dreamers' galas soars my imagination
to witness and embellish the imagery of my fabulous intentionally

Chosen well-heeled accomplished outcomes pushed the button
on my elevator raised me to my penthouse of hellacious health
windfalls of wealth feeling my passionate elegance dances with

My farseeing feelings enterprising ecstasy excites my brainpower
energizes my brainprowess opens my streams of victory as I
understand and admire my inner peace that exalts my hearten

Emotions and felicity feelings sensing my amazing incorruptible
innocence within me to appreciate and admire my internal external
and eternal landscapes gleamed my rainbows of animated imagery

Colored bright omnipresent wondermint sweetens my innerprising
inspirations to saturate my cells of celebration because my world of
words is my trailblazer savvy that gallantly glides me through

My mountains of mystery my deserts of mystical mastery my prairies
of chosen minted miracles to yacht on my oceans of sumptuous
vacationers' ecstasies surfing on my seas of splendor because

I awakened to my world of words that opened my core clairvoyant
eyes and ears to see hear taste touch smell the celebratory cosmoses
canny omnific spectacular mystique optimizes spontaneous

Enterprising savvy that awakens my spirited acumen visualizing
vibrant yazzasnazzy splendor flow through my life extravaganzas I
now admit and admire it is my and everybody's divine delights

Beams my omniscient brilliance decrees I party with my internal external and eternal playful extravaganzas within me matured exalting intuitive woo that goosed my innovative wit to spryly shit and

Get up straight thru my trials of torment smash and discharge all my worrywart walls into my silky-smooth trails of triumph as I wine and dine on my Riviera of rich relaxation titillates rabble rousing

Internal utopia matures pristine hellraisers crazy to feel wonderfully weird unleashed whimsical exuberance initiates rapturous appreciation for my fashion designer gifts that excites my inventor's scenery

As I now realize and admire weird and crazy unwinds my societized mind that swiftly unleashes my spirits sassy savvy to understand and esteem weird and crazy let's fly my feisty luminous yazzasassy spirit

Lights my fire of desire to admire weird and crazy inspirationally expresses my wisdom energizing groundbreaking robust daredevilry celebrating my royal affluence zooms yazzacashflow that

Fluently unleashes my intentionally chosen fun as I admire my fiery forerunner fortitude that unbridles my weapons of wininity executes my wise internal nerve ingeniously neon's inspiration that titivates

Yazzasnazzy sovereign heart love to instantly pulls the wheels off my past instantly fueling up my rocket as I blast off to my wild frontier of futuristic revolutionary omnific celebrations kinetically exhilarates

Trailblazer savior faire ignites my innate nunow vows of fun revolutioneyeszing omniscient nibbana treasures enlivens eternal resplendent serenity decrees I AM forever free excites and lights up

My spiritual prowess revering my bright light of inlightenmint experiencing extremely exquisite wisdom health wealth and love as I AM loved as I let go of happy to forever sensing my gladden state

Of amazing peace feeling aware of my daring dreamers daredevilry
as I AM spiritually awakened to understand and admire my words of
wisdom are mightier than the self-righteous rhetoric that sent me up

A creek without a paddle as I now realize and admit my words are
my swords of sapience cuts clean through the worrywart fences
disintegrates my snobbish scaredy cat bratiness as my vibrant

Universe spins on my words of wisdom optimizes my rapturous dawns
that beam my sunrise praises of my amazing acuity that unlocked my
world of regal luxury salsas me through my day to day experiences

As my liberated libretto opened my day to day life of thriving trendsetter
hellraisers innovative vibrancy instigating nunow gumption that
excites my knight of kinetic nirvana integrity galvanized humble

Trailblazer wizardry to flow through my adventurous veins of vigorous
enthusiastic inspired numinous serendipitous charm that disarms
my immaturity and insecurity lets fly my forthright lionhearted

Yazzabrilliance that thunderbolts my confidence and lightning bolts
my courage empowers my gut gumption to feistily face the negativity
within me and the world with noble eloquent genius acuity titillating

Visionary imagery titivates my young at heart hutzpah exalts awe-
inspiring rapturous tranquil thrill that awakened my soul self-cohesion
unlocking love within me as I now gather and declare my words are

My wonderful world of exploration through my visionary imagery of
my colorful intuition excited my painter's prowess that painted my
panorama mural of my Garden of Eden luxury appreciating loving

Life through a glowing gusto gratitude as I now realize and esteem
unsavory encounters occur the instant my fearful listening and
insecure communicative convicts were dissolved and paroled

From controlling day to day life and stealing my dreams as I allowed
outside sources dictate my life as I energized my debonair flair of my
frontiersman bravura I stopped the outside world from dictating

My day to day life to awakening my querying questionnaire verve
to ask me pointed questions instantly unlocked my unconscious
blocks instantly emancipated my innate investigator investigate as

My canny cross examiner uncovered my jackals hidden in my
unconscious landscape so I ignited my farming skills instantly
tilling out my doubting grouchy greedy seedy weeds of harassing

Herdocracy promptly shoveled out all my tormenting turdocracy as I
unshackled my innermost heckling jackals tossing them into obscurity
as I now feel my inner self worth energize my sassy classy sassy

Sovereign savant opened my eyes to my never want anything instead
I magnetize the universe with imaginative imagery and manifesting
words of wealthy optimistic revelations dawns my surpluses of lavish

Endless abundance and lush money flow I received instantly as I now
realize and admire my world of words opens my universe of utopia
unleashed my jubilant all-seeing poetic inspiration aggrandizing

My innerprising poetry to awaken my imaginative imagery energizing
my intuitive wizardry electrifying my innovative spontaneity excites
my dancing daredevilry energized my farseeing rabble-rousing

Entrepreneurial skills exhilarate my serendipitous bliss that awaken
my imagination electrifying my images and words to intriguingly
travel the world in a wonderful optimistic resplendence loving

My dreamers' paradises because I paint the murals of magnificent
ubiquitous regal animated optimist's imagery stimulating effervescent
splendor unleashing my Picasso ardor to soar of stupendous

Splendor lets fly artistic talent as I paint my life of luxurious imagery
charismatically color my heavenly skies as I witness my panorama
paradises of pristine peace and flourishing prosperity sensing

My cheery spirit of amazing grace that flows thru arteries of awesome
as I feel within me I fly free loving my lavish world of verses that
opens my gates to my endless ritzy rapture now and forever more

My life gets better and better every day in every way because I
understand and admire my world of words opens the way for
me to stroll of stunning success feeling blessed as I trusted

My innerprising prowess energizing my nunow wow exhilarates my
supernatural abilities to exquisitely entrust trailblazer talents trusting
my inventors' gifts admiring my vision of a troublemaker embraces

My trendsetting revolutionist optimizing unexampled bravery lionizing
enterprising mystique aggrandizing kevalin elegance glorifying
my rapturous intrinsic synergy embracing my stylish designs

Listening Enthusiast

I dissolved and eliminated my being a blathering talker talking slang of dang realizing and admitting I will talk my way to the outhouse listen my way to the penthouse to view my life through Shangri La

Splendor that directly energized my listening enthusiast harkens and harvests other people's wisdom as I am tutored by the wise people of the world as I experience my chosen fulfilled blessings to live and

Experience my sweet nirvana windfalls of everything dynamic that elegantly expands me through life by listening to invisible universe hearing inaudible inspirations neon's utopian daredevil intuitive

Brainprowess lionizes effervescent glistening genius lore instigating spirited trailboss enterprising nerve to clear my mountain passes for me to ride trusting my mountain man moxie and warrior wisdom

Hearing wise words of acuity from the mystical oracles of the universe that express to me because instantly stopped being a know it all talker kept me stuck inside the limits of my knowing thinking and memory

Mind that bounced me around in paucity illiteracy like a pinball stuck between two rubber bumpers bouncing back and forth in the same place never ever going anywhere always wondering why

My life never moved from yesterday because I nonchalantly romanced my past because that is what my thinking knowing memory minds identified and my recorded representations felt safe and at ease

Distinguishing I was protected because my past was easy familiar comfortable and is the map that I lived my everyday life by so I kept speaking and reliving my other world stuff as I awake to grasp and

Admit that's what I understood within minds so I swirled and twirled in days gone by stuck in spooning my other world all left me last night as my light of liberation illuminated my listening enthusiast heart

To hear entertaining acumen realizing today is the day I awesomely amble onto my divine cloud nine lightning bolts my rainbow brilliance that beamed my nunow sunrise surprised me with shrewd

Spontaneous thrillpower excited me to realize and esteem I AM a listening enthusiast expanding nowborn trailblazer honour unsheathes savant intuition actuates sassy tenacity to admit and understand

The universe let fly my nunow imaginative visionary eloquence revolutioneyeszing soothsayer enterprising wizardry via my listening enthusiast's clarity purifying my dreamers' ecstasies evicting

My vindictive inner stubbornness that kept me corralled in my bullheaded brouhahas that I watched and witnessed to be blown to smithereens instantly as I now admit and dissolve I was

Comparing myself to others and in competition with other people as I now realize and admit whenever I think I'm in competition I struggle with that situation because I am worrying about what I know and

My abilities and what they know and their abilities and are they better than me and will they do better than me was my peevish tussles going on within my inner mind's operandi's as I now realize and admit

Wisdom and inspiration are forever curious to open nunow horizons for me to adventure over to see the panorama views pristine scenery as I instantly realize and concede I am unable to listen to anything when

I compare myself to others and when I think I'm in competition my brain is busy trying to outdo other people involved trying to out think the other person I was in a conversation with so I walk away from

Any seminar or situation the same as I walked in because I walked in with an overthinking mindset of know it all unfamiliarity full of inexperience with my egoistical arrogance in high smear and

Foolish disarray that kept me dimly spinning inside my limits of yesterday yet all my boundaries of yesterday went away as I now awaken my gut courage and emotions confidence to relish NO

Articulates my Nunow Optimism unleashes Nabob Opportunities hastily expands energizes enterprises and experience as I grab the mane of dream swing aboard and ride hell bent for election

To experience my superb accomplished upshots as I yell yes to my enterprising ideas that expand everybody involved so I evolve of engendering visionary omnific lore venturing ubiquitously cherishing

My dreamers dare valiantly shows me I encompass the guts confidence and courage as I let go of being in competition thinking I had to better than the anybody never realizing and admitting I was

In competition with that person because I now admit being in competition shut off my listening enthusiasts lithe and stopped me from hearing the wisdom and gifts at whatever I was attending or

Doing in my life because to be in competition with the anybody distanced me from my highest outcomes as I now realize and concede I did that a lot in my life as I opened my wizardry eyes of wise

I witness and esteem I avow I AM awesome vibrant optimizing clever innovative wiit listening with a champion's canny hellraisers acuity magically pioneering inventor's optimistic nous stimulating

My innate unexampled talents to rise and shine within me as I ride my trails of trendsetter revelations aggrandizing inventor's lore unleashing my intuitive imagination to roam across my innovative wilderness

That expresses my nunow noesis that naturally opens enterprising savvy instigating spectacular success to bless my life as I awakened to instantly dissolved the know it all ignorance I instantly dissolved and

Liberated my listening enthusiast life escalating adventures as I participate and facilitate my enterprising endeavors energizing my geysers of fabulous fulfillmint sweetly strolls me onto my pastures

Of milk and honey that flows of tranquil vacationers' gratitude as I now realize and admit I was never ever able to listen to the wisdom of anybody thinking I was smarter and better than whoever was

Me sabotaging myself and shutting down detecting my delusional demons that were had hiding inside me as I freed me from the delusions I instantly unpolluted my inner farseeing folklore because

I unleashed my omnipresent imagination that let fly my omnific artistry that electrified my inventors innovative wiit of my wisdom inspiration and visionary talents because listening glistens gallant

Luminary intrepid trendsetter energy naturally stimulating mystical imagination that lionizes intrinsic savvy tantalizing revolutionary inborn nirvana splendor intimately yazzajazzes my hellraisers

Heart yazzapizzazzes my soul's yazzasnazzy gumption that yazzadazzles my brainpower that yazzasassies my brainprowess that wows my nunow visionary virtuoso unleashes my awesome abilities

Daredevil dexterity and seers' wisdom to listen to live internally sovereign titivating exquisite nibbana delights that brighten rainbows of colorful charisma to charm my way through life because I AM

A eavesdropper fanatically exciting my imaging guru galvanizes utopian rabble-rousing ubiquitous trailblazer bravura boldly rousing audacious victors' ubiquitous regal autonomy within me

As I majestically matured internally I double dared me to listen with
a sapient fervor escalates natural thaumaturgy harmony feeling savory
innocence glorifying zesty magnetism inside me as my ardor Zen's

My intestinal fortitude excites my emotions spine-tingling tenacity as
I AM mustang with mystical ubiquitous savvy titillating adventurous
numen nous as I AM the spiritual leader of my life with esteeming

My trailboss moxie is alive and well within me as I AM galloping
through life with the greatest of vibrant delight as I directly said yes to
the piquant grandeur of the universe as I expand graciously through

Life beaming unrestrained fame and fortune to ride my trails of
treasured riches appreciating my internal luxury now and forever more
I soar keeping the know it all mouth shut and my enterprising ears

Clear to harken the innate imagination colored shrewd visions that
glides me onto my rainbow bliss kissed my bright Life of Riley
gleaming I AM Free from me matured elegant spiritual splendor

Upshot Scenarios

I gloriously admire my utopian upshots that beams my pristine vibrancy painting my worldly vista of visionary inspirations stimulating today's amazing gifts of galvanized internal fortitude titillates classy

Sovereignty that imagines and innovates my spectacular tera incognita festivities as I now feel energized and wise to walk internally sassy every day embellishing hellraiser heart hutzpah as I love living

My utopian upshots allure my futuristic fantasies escalating amazing traveler's utopia rebelliously embellishing life's effervescent splendor as stroll thru my fulfilling I AM liberated me and the other world

As I now realize and concede the only way I dramatize and dramatize today is I bring the meme melees from yesterday and before as I unwind my al natural now that electrifies my adventurer's lore

Neon's audacious triumph ultimately revolutionizes extraordinary luck nobly optimizes wonderful heavenly heydays to be my way to me now as I now feel see taste touch smell and hear my lush endless upshot

Scenarios as I let fly my utopian power streaming hellraiser optimism tantalizing sassy clever enterprising nomadic mettle revering inspirational omnificence that steam heats my spunky trailblazer

Enthusiasm animates mystical artistic wizardry that instantly rousted out my clairvoyant gumption to let go and expand out of possibilities to expand of upshot scenarios as I expressed upshot scenarios

I instantly feel engendering excitement all through my brain pageantry that strolled me onto my red carpet of copious cornucopia as I am relaxed with adroit confidence eager and ready to ride my trails

Of victory as my ultimate wow glorified my fervent feelings and my inspired emotions to witness and feel I AM wise and energized gliding on my airwaves of brave feeling and flying fantastically free

As I my nomadic nirvana awaken within me maturing enterprising courage and innovative confidence to witness my imaginative imagery awaken my grit get and go to understand and admire my upshot

Scenarios unlocked phenomenal spectaculars troublemaker tenacity unleashed my omnific fashion designer to masterfully understand and value to expand out of my unconscious prison and survival mode

Mockery that caused me to mock and ridicule myself thinking I was ridiculing and mocking other people with follow the herd slurs of sabotage as I now awaken to admire and fathom I encompass sassy

Spine-tingling pluck to color outside the lines painting my out of this world upshot scenarios with ultra-powerful synchronized ceremonious charm harmonizes my adventurous innovations optimizing stunning

Success treasuring my flight of fancy free fulfillmint with pleasure gratitude and appreciation as I relish and embellish my stunning settings of inlightened delights that brighten life extravaganzas

As perpetual prosperous peaceful images of my dreams and chosen accomplished outcomes as I now realize and admit possibilities is endless yet lackluster within me as my upshot scenarios electrify

Adventurous action because my Picasso Prowess awakens to paint my dreamers' paradises ultrabright nirvana letting fly my omnipresent power that spurred my pacesetter poise to experience my fruitful

Endeavors because I expanded and enthused my brainpower to stream of curiosity energizing my brainprowess to decorate my universe's scintillating splendor accents my clairvoyant pictures

That thrilled my omnific imagination sparked my quick-witted intuition
animated my rabble-rousing inspiration electrifying my inventor's
innovation letting fly my trendsetter talent inspired my holidaymaker

Fortes rocketed my fame and fortune to feel my vitalized ecstasy
witnessing my easy stroll extolling my dignified triumphs that
blessed my life as my nowbirthed style invigorates and imprints

My unconscious settings with my picturesque scenarios as view
the panorama scenery of my inner universe external world and
eternal Garden of Eden that I stylishly embedded throughout

My subconscious and unconscious landscape because my upshot
scenarios energize my infinite inlightenmint intimately invigorates
nunow lore instigating gallivanting hutzpah thunderously lightning

Bolts my nowborn magical imaginative nous titillating my stroll of
plush lush prosperity as I AM sashaying on my roads of riches ambling
down my inlightened paths to witness my rivers of fluid gold bullion

That flows to me in effortless way as I now play on omni aura of
affluent utopia revolutioneyeszing ascending acumen to understand
and admire everything I desire to experience is above and brightly

Beyond everything I think and know because everything I think and
know stems from yesterday with my thoughts being brought forth
from my in-built opinionated minds as I now express to me myself

I my deep-rooted in minds that are landmines of self-taught torment
that jumps out and bites me with my delusional doubt insecurity and
immaturity so today on my third eye movie screen I play my chosen

Life of rapturous leisure magnificently basking in the sun of whatever
I desire to do at that moment as my river of gold bullion flows
forever flows to me in in a bright wonderful way as I saunter on to

My beaches of bountiful bliss watching my rivers of gold bullion flow
into my oceans of opulent opulence as I dance on my seas of stunning
success as I feel beautifully blessed because I trusted ultramodern

Sightseer cognizance that matured my peaceful warrior to hellaciously
enjoy my life of exquisite fulfillmint to experience my fun of the
sun grandeur and multicolored scenarios of my dream delights

As I now realize and admire the al natural now shows me my naked
optimistic world of wonderful opulent rich luminary dance of my
well-heeled numinous nirvana celebrations energizing my wisdom

To understand the empowering liberation of nameless blameless
shameless characterless faceless featureless unexampled and
unexplainable extravagance as I courageously embrace my radical

Thrillpower to travel effortlessly through my wild blue adventures
with audacious daredevil vigor electrifying my numen trendsetter
ubiquitous reveries energizing my spectacular al naturel now

Trusting my naked omnipotent will to trust my trailblazer resolve
unleashing my sassy torchbearer insight that cleared and endeared
me to my soothsayer savvy that unstitched my itch to bitch about

My past anybody or anything about life because my utopian spirit
shows me I am buffed exuding brilliant ultra-brilliant farseeing felicity
to celebrate my stark-naked sparkling splendor because my now is

My pure clairvoyant nowborn nous with outré spunk to understand
and admit living and experiencing my supreme energy beams me
onward appreciation upward gratitude and incorruptible love neon's

My animated tranquil utopia exalted my ceremonious elegance
naturally aggrandizing robust intrinsic optimistic stamina for me to
saunter into my fires of hell grabbing the inner delusional devil

By the nap of the neck and seat of pants tossing my delusional devil
into a warm vat of milk chocolate sweetening my delusional devil up as
I gently tossed my delusional devil into my winds of oblivion directly

Turned on my rainbow optimism coloring my world with optimist's
brilliance lionizing inventive visionary mystique exalted my unique
unsheathed triumphant rabble-rousing entrepreneurial skills

As I ride on my divine cloud nine of fun feeling unlimited nirvana
embellishing my nowborn life of Riley now and forever more I float on
my rivers of liquified gold bullion I bask on my mountains of scenic

Pleasure as I enjoy my pristine inner peace and ceremonious utopian
upshots excited my spine-tingling temerity shined sunlit utopia to
witness and esteem my portraits of I AM amazingly grand today and

Every day in every way living my dreams as my physical world is the
mural of my dreams as eternity is the light of my dream's ecstasy as I
feel my humor is alive and thrilling today and every day in every way

Au Naturel Now

I now mastered and esteem my day to day adventures are my au natural now that soared me out of yesterday to expand of my nowbirthed optimist's fortunes energizing omnific fame to glide

Me thru life touring on my winds of wisdom experiencing my au natural nirvana to ride my tides of entrepreneurial imagination dawned my electromagic mystique electrifies my spiritual spectaculars

That illuminates my roads of rad riches exhilarating sumptuous extravaganzas as I unleash my gamer gumption lets fly innerprising thrillpower that I opened honourable selfworth to grasp and concede

I clouded my today by bringing my yesteryears memories into my present moment experiences making today familiar with yesterday's episodes so I discharged yesterday to awaken my sovereign

Au naturel daredevilry jazzed my sassy tenacity that instantly liberated me from me that inspirited my intrinsic bravura escalating revolutionary animated trailmaker enlightenmint sweetens

My au naturel grandeur as I glide like an eagle over the Rocky Mountains on clear summer day relishing the panorama scenery of my life as I now look onward to gleam my au natural Shangri La blooms

My zooming bodhi light optimizes omniscient majestic maturity that sheens my pristine keen colorful inner scenery gleams my Rembrandt reveries boldly unleashed my dignified audacity that dethroned and

Emancipated the fearful bossy feelings emotions and memories that brought forth the image's opinions and viewpoints from my past that clogged up my inner workings with torment and turmoil because

I taught myself to think know and live from the familiar past that casts me in back into yesterday's way of thinking and knowing that is all gone like yesterday's dawn sprees my spiritual liberation feeling

My celestial festivities of I am alive like a beehive thriving energizing my au naturel wow embellishing my waltz of wisdom celebrations to daringly tango with my classy self-spontaneity that whirls and twirls

My bodacious dexterity thru my hellraiser heart and my rabble-rousing soul that exposed me to my barefaced optimistic world of breathtaking rainbow virtuosity that thrilled my VIP valor to dance with

My dreams astonishing festivities enthused my classy designer to sketch and color my au naturel mural of my visionary felicity that embraced my radical thrillpower to travel effortlessly through

My wild blue yonder to witness the vibrant visions savoring my present moment mystic of unique utopian lore unleashes my audacious daredevil vigor electrifying my numen trendsetter ubiquitous acuity

Electrified my spectacular au naturel gusto that glorified my naked omnipotent will to buzz my spine-tingling trust inspirited my trailboss resolve unleashes my spirited torchbearer insight that cleared and

Endeared me to my soothsayer savvy that unstitched my itch to bitch about anybody anything and the memories about the past because au naturel debonair flair streams my noble omnipotent serendipitous

Luck to celebrate my supernatural splendor because my au naturel prescience shows me my pure clear moviemaker valor ignited my ultra-gladiator spunk discharged and zoomed me out of

My unsavory flukes of abuse from the past as I now realize and concede the only abuse I really endure is the abuse I put myself thru so I airmailed all the abusive flukes to oblivion in a loving way

As I now savor my au naturel nirvana feeling my treasured love
neon's animated tranquil utopia relaxing elegantly lionizing my life of
serene leisure because I unhooked and ascended out of the stinking

Overthinking stress and all negative stuff from my thinking memory
mind disbanded and soared out of all my yesterdays uncapped
my nowborn wisdom that expanded of my idealists' affluence

To fathom and esteem my nunow wow opened my eyes of wise that
unbinded minds leaving my minds behind unwinds and let's fly native
shrewdness to shit and get down my trails of triumph unleashed

My artistic spirit to hue my native colorful clairvoyance that initiated
my Picasso talents opened my eyes heart artistry and soul designer
clarity that outlines decorates and personifies my charismatic

Breathtaking scenarios of my life's flights of panorama splendor
celebrating my classy sovereignty that rhumbas with my numinous
animated innovative wizardry established my stunning success

Feeling my fantastic fulfillmint that sweetened my exquisite posh way
of life as I thrive of frontrunner imagination accelerating my visionary
epiphanies sets my free to feel rabble rousing classy enthusiasm

Fortified my numen trendsetter mystique that gleams my
unfathomable spiritual magic facilitates my affairs of dare that
enthuses my moneymaker flair appreciating my warrior daredevilry

Frees my perky sprees of sassy perspicacity that triggers endeavoring
eloquence to flow over my vocal cords expressing canonized omnific
rhymes of my divine lexicon's dawns sunrise wizardry streams

My esteemed spiritual awakening through the earth's frequencies
of easy living effortlessly let's fly my electromagic serendipity that
magnetizes the universe breezes as I feel hear and witness

My supernatural acuity gusto's my ultimate nowborn intuitive revelations sheens electric virtuosity ascends everybody on earth out of yesterday as I now realize and admit societies ways are from

Yesterday and from a secret societies' agenda invoking their socialized mindset romancing the past people telling their dramatized stories and traumatizing insults over and over again about what went awry

In their life as they tell their stories through their victimized and pity me mindset thinking of something and somebody should take care of them for challenges because the past controls the world today I set

Myself free mastering and esteeming I am eloquently confident internally strong trusting my life escalating communicative wizardry and spine-tingling tenacity to stand up for myself with class and

With a heart vigor and a warrior soul sets free my heart hutzpah and soul chutzpah cut the crap of the past out of my life as my subconscious celebration's featureless emotions and colorless

Feelings paint my murals of magnificent utopia rapture animates loving splendor as witness the beauty of my oceans of life hear my waves of wealthy healthy taste the oceans nectars of copious

Cornucopia decorates the fluency of my financial freedom and smell my al natural ocean air of vibrant vacationers delights that brightens my inlightened inner scenery to serenely sense the sweet scent

Of mountain air feeling the sand beaches of my bountiful bliss as feel grounded throughout my life as I feel my shiny al natural now warm my inner scenery gleams my sunny glees of spiritual felicity

Whooshes my tranquil au naturel flow of I AM at pristine peace internally externally and eternally that allows me to question my present moment gifts of glorious innovative foresight tantalizing

My vanguard vitality excites founding father veracity and founding mother magnificence illuminates my au naturel inlightenmint that strolled me onto my amusement park enjoyment as I saunter upon

My Seashores of fun of the sun luxury optimizing my divine au naturel bliss that energized nunow animated nirvana celebrations invigorating today's yazzasnazzy surprises of my copious cornucopia waterfalls

Of mammoth money flow that are purposefully delivered to me today and every day in every way from everywhere in the cosmos mirroring Niagara Falls during the spring thaw as I now masterfully admire

I AM forever flowing and glowing of rare revolutionary avant-garde wisdom and supernatural talent to expand through life with the greatest of ease forever energizing adventurous savvy enjoy my life

Of Riley now and forever more I soar of spiritual optimism aggrandizing rapturous colorful heart visions to see the world as an optimistic entertaining playground of fun and relaxation

Tabula Rasa Rapture

I now master and treasure my tabula rasa rapture highlights my pure
clear backdrop I sketch color and paint my jubilees of free festivities
and my endless financial freedoms for me to show the world the way

Of revolutionary love that rapidly dawns and spawns my supernatural
phenomenon's animates fascinating fervor grandeur to flow through
my veins of vibrant sophistication invigorating nomadic spontaneity

Glorifies my grit get and go that galvanizes my celestial confidence
and bull rider courage that detached and raised me out of the
chronicled minds that stored everything from my past and controls

Me today as I masterfully admit my past events are templates
representations imprints behaviors and patterns of my other world that
naively and silently manipulates my life today so by recognizing and

Admitting this to myself I unfettered brilliant ways of expanding my
present moment gifts of gallant ingenuity discharging and soaring
me out my previous world events as I say good bye as I let fly

My tabula rasa rapture rock n rolls my trailbreaker audacity brightens
my spiritual lore enlivens my innovative risk-taking savvy embellishes
my hellraiser will to fathom and concede my daily events provokes

My yesterday's remembered thinking and memorized knowing triggers
my irked emotions miffed opinions and unsavory representations that
hide in my recorded minds that chides me into reacting every time

That type of event is activated creates the way I react or respond to
my day to day events exalts my vibrant vigor vehemently invigorates
gregarious rapport that whizzes my eloquent ardor that soars

Me thru life with the greatest of ease as I now realize and value I instantly uncovered and dismissed my fearful thoughts and tormenting thinking because I was worried about something going wrong

That created my insecurities that scurried the worry into excuses that pilfered my dreams and desired way of life as the recorded minds are the part of me that thinks feels and remembers as I ask me

How does fear and thinking I scared of something grow in to be procrastination? As I queried me as I heard my embedded worrywart templates causing me to never push beyond my boundaries

Of my fears because I now fathom and esteem my zealous vocabulary opened my subliminal savoir-faire that powered up my innate poetic poise that cleared my savvy sightseers' eyes to see my panorama

Utopias classily loving my calm vacationer's pleasures as I discovered my gold mines of miracles optimized my sumptuous utopians' mystique imagination neon's exquisite opulence because I decorated

My universe's breathtaking abundances energized and enterprized my spiritual charm bejeweled my rad rainbow mural of magnificence marvelously embracing my au naturel posh money flow zooming

My charismatic colossal magnetism relishes and embellishes my Shangri La Grandeur as I grin of rebellious appreciation naturally dawning everyday utopia glee sprees as I soar of spiritual optimism

Applauding my regal riches that lavishly and endlessly flow to me from out of my generous moneyed up cosmos as I celebrate my hellraiser holidaymaker's fun feeling unlimited nirvana

As I avow I AM awesome and amazing today and every day in every way as I realize I can never go back and fix or change anything in my past but I can expand out of my past by hearing and witnessing

My present moment gifts of genius intuition liberated me from my yesterday's torment instantly imaging nowborn illustrations of my dreamers' paradises sketched on my unconscious venues and

Subconscious festivities of marvelous fulfillment that thrilled my crisp bright realization of my au naturel nerve embraces my nowborn numen perspicacity that my au naturel life is colorless faceless

Blameless characterless voiceless unexampled unexplainable inaudible unseen and depersonalized it is me myself and I entrusting my trailblazer wizardry excites my hellraiser heart love to understand

My clairvoyant love is my powerhouse of gladiator gumption kicking my illusions and delusions to the curb then blasting them to oblivion and beyond endeared me to futuristic insight panoramic insight and

Ultrabright Shangri-La energized my seer's artistry that outlined my tabula rasa portraits beamed my inborn breathtaking scenery animates my panoramic views of my optimists' euphoria as I inspire

My prime-time enterprising ventures that flow through my third eye movie as my ravishing rapture is my cloud nine nirvana that cleared my seers' eyes opened angel ears magnetizing my golden touch

Feeling my gold bars of abundances that triggered my sovereign smell of stunning success as I taste the scrumptious splendor of my moneyed up outcomes feeling my fruitful fulfillmint tasting

My sweet nectars of nirvana as I treasure my globetrotter's poetry elegantly expresses my heart love and soul's splendor magnetizing the universes airwaves with my magnetic magnificence

To intentionally manifest my chosen life of relaxation preferred achieved upshots and vast rivers of fluid gold bullion that stream to me in an easy effortless way now and forever as my tabula rasa

Intuition fuels my state-of-the-art imagination enlivened my winds of wisdom excites my spirited inspiration exhilarates my inventors' innovations unleashed my trailblazer talents awakened to shine

My divine energized spontaneity that expands me through life to ride on my cloud nine because I now understand and esteem my tabula rasa rapture sparkles my clear slate of innate imaginative mystical

Nous animated my Pulitzer Prize Winning eloquence opened my heart eyes connecting my soul's clairvoyance to understand and admit my fears are learned behavior yet I would blame it on outside sources

As my arrogance would tell me it was never me and my snobbish conceit justified to me as my fears caused me to be coy and to shy away from everything beyond what I know as I now grasp and admit

My worn-out fears accessed my excuseopedia where my hidden excuses hid creating delusional discouragement stifled me in my blame shame narcissistic pride and know it all ignorance

As I now realize and admit my I everything I know was my current way of life yet to experience my desired outcomes I discharged my larcenist intimidating muck of mocking myself into mediocrity

Instilled my disdaining low esteem all perished from my life now in loving way as I thank you for being part of my life but now is moment for all my mocking mediocrity and low esteem BS to burn in my fires

Of freedom as my newfangled felicity masterfully admiring my unconscious omniscience dances my outré omnificence optimizes my enlightened ingenuity excites my fond bonds of bountiful bliss…

As I sassily unleashed my supernatural powers of listening to energize my divine spirit purposely manifests my lavish endless cashflow that was delivered and received in my life today and every day in

Every way because I AM the enterprising entrepreneur with skills
that thrill my risk taker tenacity to bask of unlimited health wealth
wisdom love and stylish fulfillment as I feel blessed internally blessing

My external world with innovative wisdom shining my sunny
bright spirit through eternity beaming my classy sassy selfworth
in a beautiful way I adore my liberation to deliberately enjoy

My serendipitous bliss that streams thru all phases of my amazing
life as I wholeheartedly embrace my ambling gamblers courage and
wisdom ow and forever more I soar of spiritual sapience to float on

My cloud nine divine omni aura of my magnetic animated utopian
revelation ascends my ZenZations of invisible powers of seer's savvy
unrestrained my famous supernatural electromagnetic forces are

My imagination wisdom inspiration intuition innovative talent
magnetizing the universes airwaves manifests my copious cashflow
now naturally romances my wonderful life extravaganzas

Inspiration Wisdom and Celebrations

I now appreciate and admire my life esteems inspiration wisdom and celebrations as I soar out of yesterday to experience my nunow wow of enthusiastic inspiration energized wisdom and adrenaline-charged

Celebrations as I now feel my vibration of celebrations unleashes my victorious inspirited exuberance excites my vibrant prodigies revved up my animated optimistic nerve opened my forthright sincerity thrilling

My laudable euphoric brilliance rousted out adventurous trendsetter omnificence that canonized enrapturing lore lights up my animated clairvoyant intuition optimizing numinous nirvana that streams

Effulgent inlightenmint through me instantly sweetens my gleaming gusto extolls my gallivanting vivacity excites my celestial jubilations thrills my farseeing zeal fervors my spiritual inspiration cosmic

Wisdom and hellraiser celebrations let's fly my visionary vibrations of liberation that rainbows valorous integrity colored my life with charismatic legendary legacies optimizes my miraculous Garden

Of Eden vibrancy that quickly glamourwised my ubiquitous splendor titillated my optimist's omnipotence fortified the wise of my hellraiser spirit and spiritual passions turned on my mystique magnetism

That magnetizes the universes affluent airwaves instantly brought me my lavishly endless beautiful life and my life of recreational resplendence as I now realize and concede I taught myself high

Speed without grease was the way to go nowhere scared of everything was my modus operandi talking tuff trying to bluff my way through life was my stifling rat a tat crap kept me frazzled trying to survive

As I deprived me myself and I from my desired accomplished outcomes and kept me trying to keep up with everybody in my physical world was the naysayer narcissism that kept me stuck

In the yesterday's knowing and my worrywart thinking the world and everybody were against me as I taught myself to try to fit in with societies way of life and being in the in crowd filled with wanting

To be something rather that realizing and admiring I was daringly dynamic just as I AM yet I now admit I encompassed paralyzing pride being too proud to admit and expand out of my shortcomings

So being pridefully proud trying to fit in with the in-crowd distrusting and disrespected myself internally as I taught myself to struggle and survive because I was stuck in my primal thinking and knowing

As I now understand and admit all negativity was made by follow the herd thinking and trying fit in with society left days ago as I hear and witness the universes frequencies of clairvoyant prescience enlivens

My spirit's inaudible inspiration that electrifies my tour de force foresight ignites my wanders wit optimizes my pioneering prowess that enthuses my traveler's felicity to understand and value my daily

Entertaining celebrations unravels clever engendering luminary elegance brightly reveres my adroit trial boss boldly opens sassy savvy to understand and esteem my pioneering prowess wows me out

Of follow the herd turdocracy that keeps my smelling and walking in the same old rat a tat crap that went away now because to get out of the smell and the view of herdocracy turdocracy be the lead dog

As my sassy savvy sovereign sun shines upon me I ride my trails of triumph trusting my trailblazer resolve as I AM brashly optimizing lucent quixotic mystique brilliantly optimizing my genius lore intuits

Magical bodhi omnificence that opens my nirvana insight
feeling my artistic agility that catapulted my numen nous
canonized my enterprising wizardry to flow through

My veins of visionary eloquence instantly neon's stupendous
fulfillmint sweetens my blood of virtuous vitality that
streams through heats up my thrillpower to awakened

My maestro mastery of my amazing intrinsic sapience steam
heats my clever dexterity that streams my esteemed moneymaker
megastar power to shine endeavors stamina titivating

My explorer's enthusiastic mystique energizing my optimist's
ecstasy for me to realize and admire my life of leisure
lionizes easy street living as I now express the blessings

Of my nowborn nowography letting fly my legendary artistry
of now numinously optimizing wondermint that sweeten
my trusting trendsetter talent that activate luminary

Enterprising elucidated treasures flow thru me myself and I to
fly feeling lionhearted yazzapanache thatch my crabby crotchety
control from my yesteryear's sneers of sabotaging naysayer

Effigies empty ruinous snafus of never go beyond my conscious
beliefs and narrow-mindedness were binded in everything I was
told by the outside world I did wrong gong song because

I now realize and value people want to see other people
fail so they feel good right where they are in their life the
outside world is a world of historical havoc being taught

To control people and people today use yesterday's historical
havoc to try to change directions today which forever
ends in dismay because to expand out of history

I expand energize enterprise and experience my nowbirthed nous
opens my fancy spontaneous brilliance optimizing revolutionary
acumen dawns my spawning daredevil adventurous fiery desire

That ignites my gut gumption that exalts my nowbirthed insight
revolutioneyeszing omnific nirvana gallantry to ride my tides of
gliding gumption to elegantly sauntering through day to day voyages

Entrusting my straightforward audacity buzzed my trailblazer resolve
aggrandizes internal luminous brilliance lionizes entrepreneur's
zeal enthuses my rabble-rousing inspirations that exhilarates

My innovative wisdom powered up my brainpower that lightning bolts
thunderous sovereign supremacy optimizes victor's effulgence wisely
embellishes my ingenious gallantry that clarifies my head honcho

Courage as I am lionhearted leader of my autonomous
pageantry coloring my world with tropical tranquility
of lush riches on my third eye movie screen

As I experience fame and fortune on my physical plane of
fame because I listen and witness my intrinsic innovative
with that sheens my debonair flair as I sassily unleashed

My supernatural electromagic magnetic listening to energize
my divine nerve purposely manifests my lavish endless
cashflow that was delivered and received in my life

Today and every day in every way because I AM the
enterprising entrepreneur with skill that thrill my risk taker
tenacity to bask of unlimited health wealth wisdom

Love stylish success and voguish fulfillment relishing my
streaming regal vacationers bliss of my tropical Garden of Eden
because I realize and esteem my grin of gratitude and smile

Of appreciation as I bask in the beauty of my awesome selfworth
riding on cloud nine drinking the fine wines of wealth invigorating
extravagant clairvoyant lovelore optimizes ultrabright fantasists

Confidence to flow and glow that connects my heart and brainprowess
hearing my voiceless empowering emotions nameless nirvana feeling
electrifying my brainprowess so I experience my life of abundant

Comfort with a nunow wow of whimsical opulent wisdom to expand
me through life appreciating internal keen-sighted profundity soars
me over my life explorations with enthusiastic inspiration oracle

Wisdom and ceremonious celebrations feeling my vibration my
fervent jubilations effortlessly trusting me myself and I to fly first
class beaming my sassy savvy sex appeal showing the world I AM

Who I AM sauntering through life my way and whoever has a
problem with that can kiss my classy sassy ass because I unleashed
my eloquent lionized bold Beautiful elegant awesome sassy tenacity

To relish my life of Riley as I walk through life beaming a light of
liberating love opening my eyes to treasure my wisdom inspiration and
celebrations as I treasure basking in my spiritual light of liberating

Love now and forever more I AM feeling and viewing my life of classy
celebrations expressing my life expanding wisdom and energizing
inspirations flow thru me to the world for all to see a better way

Artistic Curiosity

I now grasp and esteem my artistic curiosity let fly my electromagic
mystique that marvelously unsocietized my thinking instantly
optimized my sovereign valor to walk tall thru my daily life lionizes

My hellraiser hutzpah unsheathed my pioneering fascination
invigorated trailmaker audacity empowered my ingenious wizardry
exalted my spiritual maturity lauds my stunning fulfillmint sweetens

My life of leisure inspires fervor fun embellishes my dreamers'
paradises appreciating my keen fortitude to feel optimistic revelations
titillates innovative trailblazer ubiquitous daredevilry expands me

To fathom and esteem my day to day life is mystical confusion
that energizes my artistic curiosity optimizes nomadic foresight
unsheathes my spontaneous imaginative omnificence nobly animates

My adroit charisma initiates my supernatural flairs and farsighted
prescience that lasered focused my warrior eyes to see the invisible
splendor of my terra incognita that awakened my explorer lore

Awakened my artistic curiosity that enterprized my esteemed stylish
savoir-faire flair that charted painted and colored my unexampled
and panorama landscapes of my copious cornucopia that ascends

My revolutionary trendsetter ingenuity stimulated my trailboss
intuition canonizes luminous omnific lexicons elucidates my leadership
skills entrusted my thrillpower temerity to understand and admire

My camouflaged universe articulates mystical acumen that enlivened
my spiritual sixth sense invigorated my angelic hearing and celestial
visions stimulated my native artistry that spawns spectacular poetic

Animated designers daredevilry trusting my numen nous amplified
my leadership skills that unsheathed my artistic curiosity that
audaciously awakened me to stoutheartedly trust my nirvana spirit

To hear and witness my numinous prudence to stop trying to fix or
work on the past liberating me and everybody from the affixation of
trying fix or work on anything about yesterday and to stop training

Speaking or doing anything from the past because the past is the
memories that controls and manipulates present moment events
through my previous ingrained representations that sleep

In my submerged minds as now I realize and admire to expand out of
the past I listen and witness my daily encounters today because I now
admitted to me the same type of events of the past are occurring in

My present moment encounters and those happenstances have strict
self embedded drama that invokes stressed out in doubt overthinking
everything created the never-ending dilly dally trauma with same

Type characters and events invoking the testy reactionary retorts that
were invoked by my impulsive feelings and offended emotions that
binded me in my subconscious and unconscious representations and

Comfort zone so I dethroned and ascended out of yesterday because I
discharged the seedy needy greedy I'm right arrogance that is backed
up by the know it all ignorance that was my controlling troll flustered

Me from within about everything I thought I did incorrect ingrained
my falsified fears that scare me into hiding inside my anxieties
every time something outside of the familiar zone occurred had

Me flip-flopping around stuck in the fake and bake I heard from
yesterday that stopped me in my tracks crapping my pants whining
and crying about my life situations that created my today because

My past manipulated me forever until I discharge and rise out
of all the self-taught torment that created the saddening stress
always trying to live down to somebody else's fears and scaredy

Cat bratiness as I now start to laugh at my gaffs by taking the name
and face away from any event that is anchored by what was said in
the event so whatever occurs in any event say it in 12 words or less

Twelve words cuts out the delusional drama and trauma and stops
the revengeful thinking within me as I become amused watching the
arrogance and ignorance within me go away to instantly realize

The world crawls around in a pool of arrogant poopy do always
bitching and bellyaching about what somebody did and how I was
going to get even was the blemished arrogance of my ignorant trolls

That tried to steal my life as I now realize and admire I appreciate my
life and all the events with gratitude as there is zippo unsavory people
from the past in my life today as my past is now faultless shameless

Characterless colorless and faceless because I depersonalized my
recorded programing that told me it was easier to give up and be
a people pleaser than be thee expeditor of my wisdom and

Inspiration to expand people's lives as I now brashly concede and
understand I was going thru the motions of everything stopped
yesterday because I embraced my gut gall to admit and

Realize I AM accountable and responsible everything that happened
in my life good bad or uninteresting let's fly my shrewd wizardry
and trailblazer tenacity that strolled me onto my Promised Land

By trusting my enlightened warrior as I now animate my life of
Riley flying on cloud nine as I let fly my majestic freedom feeling
rich and robust as I courageously and confidently express and

Confess my wisdom inspiration and gratitude blazed my
enterprising paths of inlightenmint thru my today's encounters
by trusting my artistic curiosity that adventurously lionizes

My lionhearted unadulterated grit get and go electrified my rebellious
fortitude invigorated my numen gumption launches optimistic
revolutionary enterprising endeavors forever I energize and

Magnetize my lavish endless cashflow as glow of nowfound
understanding and confidence to look in my mirror of forever liberation
that lights up my internal brilliance energizing regal insight entices

Intrepid optimism because I now realize and esteem my biggest
challenge for me to overcome and expand out of my self-sabotaging
stubborn self-taught stuff so by admitting this I instantly stopped

Flopping around like a fish out of water as I yachted away in a bright
wonderful way as I instantly opened my invincible heart and cleared
my sassy soul unleashed my artistic curiosity to fathom and

Esteem my electric spiritual mystique is the key to my inner heavenly
kingdom feeling my magnetic kevalin energy shines my amazing
futuristic felicity that streams my esteemed enterprising elegance

Beaming my spirited smile that excites my entrepreneurial acuity
instigating innovative questioning escalates my enterprising eloquence
showing my inventors talent to world as I awakened my wisdom

Innovation inspiration and talent as I utilized to expand out of
that challenge yet to expand out of the next situation I receive
fresh foresight to ignite bright bold venturesome veracity excites

My spunky glistening listening adheres me to my nunow sightseer
acumen to taste my bountiful key lime pie in the sky success smelling
the fresh air of my debonair flair touching my mammoth mountain

Of magic embellishing my spiritual maturity understanding and admiring my unseen unexampled and unexplainable cosmos rockets me my nunow lavish endless blessings of self-realization sweetened

My heart love and my peaceful prosperous celebrations understanding and admiring the fire in my gut gallantly unleashed my trailblazer tenacity to stroll down trails of triumph to elegantly express

My imaginative inspirations that turned on my alluring inquisitive inquiries of me myself and I energized my artistic curiosity opened my adventurer's drive enlivened my grit get and go painting

My emotions murals of moneyed up gifted results and lavish endless abundances on my third eye movie screen that repeats my stunning splendor to me as my physical world magnificently mirrors

My inner scenery as I bask of beautiful serenity and bountiful bliss kissing my bountiful life good morning and good night now and forever more I soar of spirit optimism appreciating sovereign gratitude

Spirit Charm

Infinite Spirit I now admire and value my spirit charm that sheens my pristine instinctive resplendence incites tranquility calmly harmonizes amazing rapturous miracles that are purposefully chosen to deliver

My heaven on earth extravaganzas as I celebrate my life's luminous inspirations fervors entrepreneurial skills that animate my magnetic charisma unleashed my untamed cosmic tour de force to feel

My futuristic optimistic ritzy celebrations energize hellraiser audacity revolutionizes magical miracles to intentionally and instantly appear from everywhere glorifying my life of glamorous gusto

As I live internally free every day in every way as I play on my panoramic pastures of eternal peace and endless lush prosperity as I AM aware of the dare of my spirit charm supernaturally adorns

My adventurous rabble-rousing maverick sass tells all the naysayers of the world to kiss my classy brass and hastily disarmed all the harming haunts within me and the world as I now saunter of spiritual

Autonomy that unsheathed nomadic temerity to understand and admire my soul lore opened my wanders mettle to understand and esteem my majestic enterprising triumphant trailblazer lore bared

My untutored and undomesticated scenarios let fly my spine-tingling imagination wisdom innovation inspiration intuition and trailblazer talents that thrilled my risk taker flair of dare that saddled up

My mountain bred mustang unleashed my stallion stamina to ride with humble pride across my terra incognita landscapes with the fiery spirit of lead mare the speed of thorough bred that won my Kentucky

Derby the agility of cutting horse the savvy of calf roping horse
athletic ability of a barrel racing horse the power of a team roping
horse and the breakaway ability of steer wrestling horse to showcase

The pageantry of my inborn festivities that beams my National
Finals Rodeo shows my amazing achieved outcomes that is on repeat
on my third eye movie screen with representations of my victor's

Vitality and mammoth endless cashflow as I AM thee All Round
Winner of my life Rodeo that streams my intentionally chosen moneyed
up accomplished outcomes and my amazing achieved upshots I enjoy

From my physical plane of fame feeling awesome magnetically
energized as my esteemed steamy spirit charm and my gamblers
curiosity stoutheartedly strolls me thru my challenges and chaos are

The domestic jokers for me to have fun my thinking knowing and
memories kept the stuck in the muck traumatized torment and
dramatized delusional despair that perished from my life now

As I unleashed my infinite indigenous intuition thrilled my investor
tenacity instantly set me free to give thanks for my spirit charm that
electrifies my wise to realize and value my intrinsic divine design

Dawns extravagant stupendous inspirited grandeur naturally
clarifies my clever clairvoyance celebrating life animates my intrinsic
revolutionary visionary omnificence yazzajazzes autonomous nerve

Chartered my engendering grit get and go to understand and concede
my spirit charm invigorates numen trailblazer resolve intrepidly
galvanizes undomesticated enterprising ventures to be placed on

My path of infinite inlightenmint liberating me from my thinking
knowing self-taught memories and self-inflicted torment because I
now realize and admire magical curiosity inspiration wisdom and

Gratitude fly me above the fray of my life allows me to never fall
prey to my self-taught pity me palaver that I now realize and admit
internally controlled me so I sassily surrendering and dismissed

The messes of my life that instantly liberated me from me to instantly
feel and witnessed my savvy yazzapizzazz empowered my gusto
emotions that enterprized my majestic mojo optimized omnific

Nirvana excited my innate potentate prowess that powered on my
vanguard foresight to understand and laud I turned on my powerhouse
of sapient spunk to get and admit in debate with others I invent

New razor-sharp savvy that energized my spiritual maturity lighting
up my trials of pacesetter poise as I feel my emotions marry my spirit
charm undoing the poo in the stew of never do thinking awakened

My nowfangled nous to understand and concede I think know and
remember the unsavory events of my life created the ways I stay
stuck in the pity me thought then recalling the pain and agony

Of my self-taught torment creates my inner dialog that bogged me
down in yesteryears sneers as I now understand and admire my life is
traveling and sightseeing through my terra incognita phenomenon's

Let's fly my fantastic foresight ignites my infinite noble genius
ESP untamed my inborn trendsetter yazzapanache as I entrust my
trail boss lore embellishes my tracker wizardry as I daylight and

Illuminate my roads of riches through my moneyed up terra incognita
mountains is me uncovering and discovering straightforward
lionhearted confidence and stouthearted courage to explore

My entrepreneurial scenarios that bloom and boom my moneymaker
moxie that robustly rainbows my colorful charisma radiantly
highlighting my inborn unexampled wisdom unexplained inspirations

Peerless gratitude and unseen awesome achieved outcomes as I celebrating unleashing stupendous jetsetter talents that energize my life extravaganzas to understand my dreams and desired achieved

Outcomes are above and beyond everything I know that I learned from the school system societies delusional ways and mundane day to day life as my colorful gladiator bravery valiantly opened my eyes

Of wise to fathom and esteem my spirit charm is my utopian acumen and undomesticated nerve instigated my vibrant elegance revving up my spicy zeal to listen to my spirit charm that discharged and

Soared me out of the self-taught thinking trying being afraid to go beyond my thinking knowing memory minds and go beyond anything I have ever done or experienced so all my having to know before

I do anything left me dizzily whizzing on the side of the road realwising I know my way to yesterday so that exited my life yesterday that instantly endeared me to my stylish intuition that opened my eyes

Of wise and seers' ears to revere and value inspiration and wisdom are my vibrant vitality that opened and energized seers' sagacity to grasp and esteem my spirit lets fly sassy powerful ingenious revelations

Inspired trailblazer fortes of farseeing optimistic reveries tantalizing enterprising safaris as I unleashed my spirit charm imaging nirvana treasures revolutioneyezing my artistic genius that unrestrained

Energetic enthusiasm that buzzed my forthright fortitude to understand and admire my spirit facilitates my innate prowess as my spirit charm facilitates and participates with me as I effortlessly

Travel down my trials of triumph with astute curiosity canonizing utopian reveries purified my outré omnificence of untaught quick-witted clairvoyance that awakened my ultra-powerful innovative

Imagery that presented me myself and I with my well-heeled cultivated results as I AM my basking of my sun of the fun sovereignty with daring decrees of free as I dance fluently canonizing dazzling

Epitomizing eloquence steam heats my spirit's charm within me invigorate esteemed selfworth and spine-tingling respect for my stupendous ability's pristine inspiration panorama wisdom and

Healthy wealthy appreciation for my life as I now fathom and esteem my dreams matured riches to be my way of life as I bask on my beaches of princely prosperity and rainbow beauty as my luxurious

Bliss kissed me today and every day in every way as my spirit leads my body energizes my dance of liberating lore loving who I AM beaming my amazing spiritual maturity now and forever more

As I soar of spirit charm to treasure my glorious gusto galvanized my utopia splendor that streams thru me like a river flowing to the ocean on a warm summers' day so I feel my unique mystique in a bold way

Appreciation and Gratitude

I energized my day to day life through appreciation and gratitude as I unleash my appreciation that adventurously opened my heart to sense the vibrant value of all my life situations as my gratitude beams

My grin of Iwon with internal wondrous optimistic nirvana awakened my soul to send out unselfish love liberating me from me to mature majestic elegance as I dance with my life events that electrifies

Visionary epiphanies neon's trendsetter gratitude galvanizes rapturous animated trailblazer imaginative treasured ubiquitous dreamers engendering thrillpower titillates hellraiser reveries invigorates

Luminesce lore purposefully optimizes winsome electromagic resplendence to understand and concede through appreciation and gratitude I energize my nunow wow to waltz of wanders will thrilled

Me to write and experience the bright inlightened nowography of my life's nirvana omnificence whizzes optimist's gumption revving up adventurous pep hellaciously yazzajazzes my grit get and go

To saunter down my trails of triumph to bask of beautiful leisure foresure as I intentionally chosen to walk down hill to feel the frills of easy street sauntering with gratitude and appreciation as I expanded

Of optimized foresight to facilitate and participate with my venturous audacity to experience my uncomplicated life of vacationers delights that lit up my beaches of bountiful bliss that kissed me with

My fancy free living my luxurious life as I now feel appreciation ascends my audacious personalized prowess realizing expansionism canonizes inborn awareness titillating intuitive optimism neon's

My colorful charm to understand expansionism is inside me I am
free feeling my intuitive spiritual maturity energized my internal
spontaneous miracles awakens imaginative mystique intuits

Spectacular magic innovates stupendous moneymaker inspirations
stimulated my appreciation for my ability to listen to expand my
life extravaganzas thru appreciation and gratitude that turned off

The noise of the past powered up my free streaming liberation of
gratitude awakening me to fathom and esteem I appreciate every one
of my life events for their unique nowborn foresight wisdom and

Innovative wit as I confidently and bravely chosen to hear my
enterprising expansionism of innovative sagacious maturity I attained
and expanded of from every situation and every person involved

In my life events so I evolved out of my unique life events with
thankfulness and escalation as I now realize and esteem my daily
voyages bring forth tutors and metaphors that expanded me out

Of yesterday to hastily amplified my inventive prowess to experience
a bigger bolder brighter stroll onto my Broadway of posh prosperity
as I deliberately received the liberation and wisdom to expand out

Of everything and anything I thought about anybody lovingly
dissolving everybody from my life with grace and grit as I energized
my gratitude to enterprise my skills that thrilled me to grab

The reins of my fame and fortune ventures with vigor electrifying
numinous groundbreaking rapturous enlightenmint that sweetened
my heart love to concede every one of my life events were

To intensify my vim and vigor to explore my dreamers' paradises
with a sightseer savvy moviemaker curiosity gladiator audacity and
moneymaker wizardry as I awakened today to the liberating power

Of depersonalizing past by making the past faceless blameless characterless and nameless as I was mediated this morning I set myself free to entrust my aware daring charm that drew and painted

The images of my dreamer's paradises on my third eye movie screens that awakened my clairvoyant artiste to outline and design my featureless skies with my nowborn breathtaking views of my Garden

Of Eden splendor embellished my divine nirvana that embraced my nunow wow that opened my heart hutzpah that electrified my sassy valiant self-love that nobly rouse within me that exalted my waltz

Of wealth festivities opened my innocent innovative insight and self-respect to understand and value every life event expanded my wisdom audacity and talent as I awakened to disconnect my listless worn out

Insecurity and immaturity trying to hold onto the person and everything involved trying to stay inside my chronicled minds comfort zones are now gone like yesterday dawn as I instantly harked

My verve that instantly discharged people that tried drag me down to their level as I now realize and admit selfish ignorance controls the world and the beliefs of people now as I grasped and liquated

My yesterday selfishness in wonderful way as I showcase my sovereign gratitude and autonomous appreciation as my past is discharged and cleansed all disloyal people and unsavory events out

Of my life through appreciation authorized me to feel the liberating power of my spiritual maturity and sovereign selfworth by turning off the noise of annoyance and expanded them into being faceless

Nameless blameless colorless and depersonalized that detached and released me from them and liberating them from me in loving way as I instantly let fly my numen nerve that opened my nowbirthed

Acumen to understand and admire I dissolved forgiveness from my
life experiences to ascend of appreciation because that allowed me to
hear witness taste touch and smell the spirited splendor of my divine

Grandeur from the situations surrendering all the unsavory crap to
the sewers of oblivion as I live on my beaches of serene splendor and
tranquil treasures that unbinded my chronicled minds to speedily

Unwind my divine daredevilry as I am free feeling my supreme
vivacious elegance flow through veins of fame as my arteries of
artistry sketched exhibited enterprized decorated and hued

My nowborn rainbow glow of esteemed selfworth on the universes
canvases of celebration appreciating nowfangled adventures seeing
my life through my colorful charismatic lure of my dharma charm

That dawns my dauntless hellraiser audacity revving up my
amazing nunow wow avows my wonderful optimism triumphs my
wonderful bountiful beauty to stream through me to the world

That sheens my pristine panoramic views of my dreams that float over
my third eye movie screen imprinting my lush achieved upshots on
my heavenly skies and on my universe's horizons because I colored

My world my way as I entertain my fame and fortune allowing people
and events to come and go as I throw a party of detachmint feeling
sweet surrender within me decrees I intentionally received and feel

My appreciation and gratitude feeling my loving self-assurance
because the only way anything or anybody has an effect on me is
I allow it and fall prey to the victimeyetice crapeyetice and that

All went away to crash and burn in compost pile going from rat a
tat crap to futuristic fertilizer as I feel ultra to the universe I shine
my emotion's splendor now and forever more as I now understand

I AM grand magnifying my grinning rapturous aura naturally
dawning my internal external and eternal sunrise splendor that gleams
my esteemed smile of surrendering all my yesterday's to oblivion

As I energized my optimized omnipotence that geysers my nowbirthed
lavish endless life of rest relaxation and regal riches as I sovereignly
sit on my throne of inlightenmint as my crown of spirited galas

Instantly excites my numen eminence revering genius yazzapizzazz
that spiritually spurred me to naturally understand and admire
everything in my life is momentary as I raise my flag of victory

My spiritual voyager breathes my spirit strength thru my core courage
heart confidence soul's savvy and dreamer's dexterity that escalates
nowborn supernatural eulogies as I AM blessed sensing blissful love

Now and forever more as I now understand and admire my rambling
rabble-rousing gumption applauding my spirited moxie strolling thru
life with my head high shoulder back walking tall having a ball

Spiritual Nowography

I awakened to fathom and esteem my here and now is all there
is unleashed my numen omniscient wisdom that articulates and
writes my spiritual nowography soared me out of my past to love

My present moment gifts of grandeur innovating financial treasures
spontaneously energized my spiritual nowography by naturally
opening my wonderful optimist's gumption reveres adventurous

Perspicacious high-spirited yazzapizzazz sashays me on to my heaven
on earth extravaganzas as I sing my songs of my nunow nirvana as I
now detached and liquated romancing the past and making the past

Nostalgic being brainwashed by thinking and knowing trying to live
today with my past representations that manipulate today as I wanted
to change so I thought I had to change and fix my past and tell

The stories of the past that cast the shadows of yesterday in my
present moment experiences yet when an identical event of the past
occurs today instantly triggers the imprinted chronicled minds

That activates the attached feelings and emotions that control me
without me having a clue as the feelings and emotions are attached to
that type of incident starts the fury of the first event so I dethroned

The thoughts thinking knowing and living my life thru the memories
of the past that I cast into my fires of freedom as I now walked out of
my past into a waterfall of freedom that cleansed and washed the past

Out of the chronicled minds conscious mind and all my unsavory
recalls that I washed away down my stream of sovereignty to paint my
present moment magic on mystical brain of fame to feel awesome

Marvelous eloquence voicing blooming brilliance coloring my dreams
and desired achieved outcomes with lyrics of love yazzajazzes regal
imaginative ceremonious splendor as I instantly dethroned my past

To stop telling the stories about my past and the struggles of the self-
taught turmoil swiftly greased the airwaves of the universe for my
other world turmoil to leave me instantly in a loving way to speak

Write and experience my spiritual nowography that naturally
optimized winsome numinous omniscient wanderer's optimism
galvanizes revolutionary animated pioneering hellraiser yazzasnazzy

Pizzazz jazzes up my present moment magic as I now get up in the
morning with a ultrabright brilliance shining from my core chandeliers
that lights up my heart lore and soul savvy ignited my troublemaker

Mystic miraculously articulates gumptious insightful celebrations that
jumpstarts my day with jovial utopia mystically propels sunlit grit get
and go to understand and admire my fiery fervor vigor to fathom

The power of my nunow wow never ever lets me sink back into the
rinky dink stories with langsyne jargon about every that jerked my
chain of pain stained my life from yesteryear's sneers jeered me into

Reliving my past nostalgia since that's what I knew and thought as
that is what I taught myself from trying to model my everyday life to
fit in with what everybody else was doing was the glue of never do

Dawned my nowfound fortitude to realize and concede I tried to
make my past nostalgic by embellishing yesterday's stories to make
my egotistical arrogance to feel dominant over everything as I tried

To hide the stymieing strained pain of yesterday only to realize and
concede yesterday's stressful stories are my worrywart Tories today
trolling the inner scenery that manipulates the anxiety keeping

The worrywart retorts working so I purposefully chosen to discharge to oblivion that swiftly turned on my gut grit get and go to stop talking thinking knowing and doing anything with the tormenting turmoil

Of the stories of the past that instantly powered on my light of present moment mystique to understand and esteem I speak write and feel my deliberately chosen stylish achieved lifestyle that expanded me out

Of my daily routines to shine my soul nirvana that woke my risk-taking words that animated kinetic enterprising nous energized daredevil dexterity to daylight engendering Xanadu electrifies rebellious

Imaginative trendsetter yazzapizzazz as I whimsically write and jovially experience my spiritual nowography unbridled my nunow wow avows my adventurous vibrancy opens wonderful splendor

That streams thru me unleashed my spiritual sprees of free as I feel rapturous energy electrify my nowborn brilliance is my instantaneous innovative nous naturally opening unexampled savvy gifting

My inborn gumption to expand me of present moment mojo instantly trusting my adroit acuity to stroll me through life to brightly write and elegantly experience my spine tingling nowobraphy realizing and

Admiring my life is experienced expanded energized and enterprized my sparkling moviemaker charm lets fly my sprightly wise imagination wisdom inspirations intuitive innovations inventors' treasures

That awaken my nomadic young at heart hellraiser trailblazer crazy sassy classy sexy stylish swashbuckler humor appreciating my grit get and go that beams my grinning optimism and smiling spontaneity

That inspirationally expresses to the world I'm never a bragger because I showcase I AM a savvy swordsman with an illuminated sword of sapience that instantly cuts through the rat a tat crap

Of opinionated burping BS and the world's stress because I am blessed
with bold lionhearted spunk and entrepreneurial determination
to walk thru my fires of hell with a bucket of water scaring

The hell out of my internal and external devils as I witness my
delusional illusional devil run over the hill to spill into obscurity
as I rebelliously dance effervescently illuminates my sassy classy

Life and my moneyed up universe as I invigorate my rabble-rousing
visionary epiphanies stylish nowborn nowography birthing their new
way of life instantly I am brashly blazing trails of torchbearer triumph...

Wisdom naturally invigorating nomadic gumption to forever listen and
witness the universes nunow wow to waltz of wisdom electrifying my
world of wondermint expressing My sweet inspirations exhilarating

Inventors' innovations and megastar talents to understand and
admire I AM thee ultrabright maestro produced my magical movie
of my stylish spiritual nowography that lionizes eternal freedom

As I now grasp and admit I AM the maverick magician exudes miracle
grandeur excites my nowography audacity that cleared my veins of
fame that opened my hearts inspiration soul's innovations and core

Valor to admit and admire I lived through everything to write and
experience my nowborn nowography feeling my nunow spunk
dissolving all my yesterdays to understand and admire anything

That occurs within me is happening bright now that illuminates
my pathfinder's fortitude pacesetter spunk and trailblazer vitality
that amorously adheres me to my selfworth that shows me and

My celebrating cosmos my wonderful optimistic rapturous trendsetter
hutzpah that unleashes my nowfound frisky risk takers veracity
excites my numen courage and numinous confidence that thrilled

My listeners enthusiasm that hearken my hellraisers hutzpah trusting
my trailblazer troublemaker to open my trails of triumph as I stroll
down to my beaches of panorama peace looking out over my oceans

Of bountiful bliss as I kiss my Pulitzer Prize winning nowborn
nowography good morning good afternoon and good night as I shine
my bright illuminated heart gallantry invigorating natural trailblazer

Tenacity instigating optimists' nerve to never swerve or sway away
from my challenge's chaos or unsavory untimed situations because I
AM ornately rich thru my visionary vigor electrified my space-age

Inborn verve displays my intrepid athleticism and astute leadership
that will forever unsheathe my breathtaking bliss kissing my life
of Riley treasuring my rich milk chocolate flights of delights

Now and forever more I effortlessly float through my milky way of
wealth enjoying my state-of-the-art life of lush leisure ambles me thru
anything and everything onto my beaches of peaceful pleasures

About the Author

I am Robert A. Wilson with Cowboy Wisdom Hypnoacuity that Features Wisdom and Fun. As I am an Inspirational Speaker, Hypnoacuitist, Dream Sculptor and published author. Hypnoacuity matures your unconscious and subconscious celebrations. As Hypnoacuity, NLP and dreamer's freedom wisdom, rhyming poetry energizes your inspirational intuition opening enterprising expressions allows you. To realize you encompass the imagination wisdom intuition innovation and talent to experience your dreams and desired accomplished outcomes.

I give free consultations for Personal Growth, Pain Management, Weight Management, Fears, Smoking Cessation, Inner Liberation, Dreamer Freedom, and Undresses your stress to be blessed with Hypnoacuity, NLP, Parts Integration, Visionary Vocabulary and Walk of Wisdom Seminars. Acuity means sharpness of vision and the visual ability to resolve fine detail. Acuity opens the way for you to be free of the therapy.

I introduce you to the liberating power of expand, energize, enterprise and experience higher quality life. expand out of your past in present moment and **everything** occurs *now*. So, stop romancing the past and rise out of your thinking knowing and memory mind to illuminating your paths of inlightenmint riding your trails of triumph to bask on your beaches of bountiful bliss.

Robert A. Wilson
Cowboy Wisdom Hypnoacuity

Website: http://mycowboywisdom.com
Author Page: www.amazon.com/author/robertawilson
Author Page: www.howdiditeachmyselffear.com
Email: Robert@mycowboywisdom.com